STEPS FROM THE BEYOND

About the Author

The Writer of this book wishes that little be said about herself, in spite of her many physical accomplishments. She considers only that she is used as the Instrument of the Message and Teachings given here.

The Writer succeeds, with clarity, in giving answer to many vexing questions, unexplained by the various media, which have left people full of bewilderment and anxiety as to Life, its Meaning and Purpose, and further, what happens after this Life.

She adheres very strictly to The Master's injunction "TO TEACH AND HEAL". The importance of these Teachings cannot be overestimated, and it must be emphasised that the WORK OF GOD cannot be circumscribed in any way.

In spite of all manner of difficulties, she has devoted her life in Selfless Service to Mankind.

A small token by One who thanks God for the Blessings of Light and Healing received through this Instrument.

N.S.

STEPS FROM THE BEYOND

MARGARET GALLOWAY

ELEMENT BOOKS

First published in Great Britain 1976
This edition first published in Great Britain 1986 by
Element Books Ltd
Longmead, Shaftesbury, Dorset

ISBN 0 906540 87 9

Printed in Great Britain by
Billings, Hylton Road, Worcester

CONTENTS

Steps from the Beyond

CHAPTER 1

WHAT AM I?

There are hundreds and thousands of people living in the World today, who constantly ask themselves the questions—What am I? Why am I living? What is the meaning of life? Is there any purpose?

As a Nation, we believe in the power of the Christ, and follow, if we are true Christians, the Doctrines that are contained within our Bible. We have also to remember that this Book was first of all given by word of mouth and later transferred to paper. It has been translated and re-translated into hundreds of languages and it is no wonder, therefore, that we find words that do not always express what is really implied, and whole phrases also, that seekers after Truth, question very seriously.

We are told that "God made Man in His Own Image". We are therefore a part of that Force and the Spirit of God is within and around us, and we can never be separated from that Love.

Many teach that the Spirit is also the Soul, but, from all I have experienced I would say No! The Spirit is of God, untouchable, pure and perfect, and can never be sullied by anything physical. The Soul is the Progressing part of ourselves, seeking evolution and knows all about itself from the beginning of its existence, or Breathing Forth, knows what it wants or wishes to attain, realises its weaknesses, but in spite of everything desires experience in the schoolroom of the World, for the exact purpose of Evolution.

The Soul and the Spirit together we know as the Etheric Body which has a life of its own, that is separate from the physical body during the hours of sleep. During the day, the physical body is as the horse one rides, or the vehicle of expression through which the Spiritual self i.e. the Etheric Body functions.

You will say immediately, "Why should we believe this, since we cannot see it"? Well, remember "Doubting Thomas", remember also, that although the sun has a corona of flames, and we cannot see it, nevertheless, we believe it because the scientists tell us so. Do we believe that the whole world is a Vibratory Force, that nothing is solid as it appears to the physical eye? Further do we believe what the Master Himself said "In my Father's House are many Mansions"? Do we believe His Resurrection and what of His Words "Blessed are they who have not seen and yet believe"? You cannot see the waves of Vibrated Force that convey our Radio Programmes or the Pictures and Sounds of Television but they have always been there.

Man has, in this age of Aquarius, been able to control these Forces, but there are many others over which he has no control as yet, nor are they yet discovered. In God's good time and not that of Man's will they be shown to him. Whether he uses them for good or ill is his own responsibility, together with the resultant effects upon the World and its people.

Man then, is a Spiritual Being, first and foremost. He is Spirit, which is of God, he is Soul, which is the Vibratory clothing of the Spirit and the part which is usually seeking progression, he is body, which is purely physical, with a brain and a mind, which can be trained and used only in so far as it has been taught to think and to respond.

When the Etheric or Soul and Spirit Body has performed the work which it came to Earth to carry out it will depart from the physical body and the process which we call Death ensues!

Many people are afraid of Death, but I sometimes feel they are not so much afraid of the actual happening, but more, perhaps, the approach to it! Those of us who have had the great privilege of watching the Etheric Body leave the physical body at Death, or perhaps see it linger over the body during a period of unconsciousness know, without any shadow of doubt, that there is that part of us that will never die, and that it will return to the Planes of Being from whence it came, on the dissolution of the physical body, NOT to become completely inactive, or as was taught so long ago, to become an Angel and play a harp, but will return to its own individuality, and continue, by the Soul's own desire, the work which was commenced on Earth.

Man, however much we would like to think it, does not become an angel in a moment of time—i.e. at his passing from the physical body. He will not be one iota different. Many people wish, while they live, to develop the Gifts of the Spirit, and think that they should be able to acquire them very easily. Such is not the case. If you wish them, then you must work and work hard, or you will gain nothing and no-one can give them to you. You, yourself, can either make or mar the progress of your own self, and you must aim spiritually high to get the best results. The great thing is to sustain the effort made. It is very easy to commence a thing, but the steadfast holding to the purpose is that which counts most of all.

This will not be easy, for once you have determined on a certain path of action, you will find that all kinds of difficulties will soon present themselves. Things that people never think of become obstacles in the way of progress—the outlook begins to change, and people appear differently. The world takes on a different aspect, but this is really not true! It is you who are changing. You are seeing things in a different light. You are learning to express yourself in a truer way. You are developing the Soul-Force within you, and the Soul is finding for itself a more ready channel of expression. It is at this point, when the Soul has stirred and is ready to fight, that the chela or pupil is usually brought into touch with a Teacher, who will gradually unfold the Higher or Inner Wisdom, for always "When the pupil is ready, the Teacher is found"! The pupil will be taught only as much as he can take, or absorb and use, and he will be watched in ways unknown to him by the Teacher, who will eventually know the signs of advancement, or otherwise, as time goes by. He will guide him gently all the time, making no decisions for him and allowing him perfect freewill at all times. The chela or pupil will often make many bad mistakes, but these in turn, will render him a service in that they will teach him by experience.

At this stage, he will begin to look at people, not entirely with the physical eye, but more with the eye of Spirit. He will regard people as Souls, in the process of Evolution, each one different, and working along different lines. Remember there are no two vibratory forces in the world that are quite the same and, therefore, no two people are the same! Having realised this, it is perhaps easier to help others. We begin to notice others, less fortunate than ourselves, more powerful or richer than we, but here again, we have to remember, that if one has power or money, or possessions, the Soul will be tested as to its use of these gifts in his lifetime. If we have any of these physical gifts we must consider them only as lent to us, for a brief period of time, and what we do and how we use them is very important indeed. There is a reason for everything that we have and are, and we must give an account of our stewardship one day. It behoves us therefore to use our gifts of all kinds, properly and in a way befitting the God who bestowed them upon us.

Let us always and forever remember that man is already a Spiritual Being, made in the Image of God, that he is composed of Spirit and Soul—the Etheric Body, that part of him that is indestructible and immortal. Remember, that this Etheric or Immortal part of God, and man, is using, for the express purpose of Evolution, a body of flesh, and that when man has finished using it, he (the Etheric or TRUE SELF) will discard it. The body will then disintegrate. The True Man, which is the exact replica of the physical body in form, is immortal, is of the Essence of God, and a Spiritual Form.

Chapter 2

SERVICE, OR SEEK YE FIRST THE KINGDOM

There comes a time in the life of a chela or pupil when he desires to give active service. Sometimes, he hesitates to take the step that would lead to his preparation for that Service.

Much work is waiting to be done in the world, but so often the desires of self make the chela withhold his service and often he does not realise the fulness of the opportunities that present themselves. Then comes the great question! Is it to be to help in the great work that is waiting to be done, or will the self and its desires come first? Will you wait, as you so often say, until the material conditions are as you think they ought to be, or will you follow the examples of those who have given themselves in TRUE SERVICE to work in the faith of Fulfilment of His Words "Seek ye first the Kingdom of the Father, and all else shall be added unto you".

If you meet all your testings and trials in brave and steadfast faith, in the Love and Guidance of the Father—Mother of all Life, and if you ask the guidance for your actions in the example of the Master's Life, *then* you will go forward to still greater and higher things; but, you will need strength and the True Force of Will, for, as the Higher Vibratory Forces cannot be used in the Planes of Earth, unless there are the Vessels through which to pass then it demands that such vessels must be selfless.

Where the self enters in, the Force of the Christos is shut out. You must then empty yourselves of discontent, self seeking possessiveness, and all the weaknesses that tempt you from the Path. You know what many thousands do not, that every movement of your body, every sound you make, every thought you conceive in your minds, is what is making, or creating the vibrations in your world today. If they are of God and His goodness, then you are bonded with the Forces of Light in the overcoming of the NOT-GOOD; but if self comes first, then are you creating the lower, or NOT GOOD VIBRATIONS.

Strive, ever to follow His Path—to be of Truth, to stand firm against those powers that would overthrow you. It is no use to say you cannot. That is but to say that you do not know your own powers of Creation. Hold in your minds, what you have so often been taught, that when you say "I will" and mean it in your hearts, then can be poured into you, and through you, all the Force of Service to Mankind that is possible and necessary for the evolving of the Soul in the Earth World.

Do you know the joy of finding a Server, or a dedicated one, seeking, at all times, and in all conditions, to be ready to work for the evolving of the Soul in the Earth World. This opens up a vast field of Service, but such a one is rare indeed.

So often channels that should be free and open for use are blocked by some vibratory force of the self, and another way must be found, or await the opportunity when the channel is again made clear. Would you think more often of this? You people of the Earth Plane are always so eager to obtain help from the Spirit, that you forget that they, too, are eagerly seeking your blending into their Force, so that they may do their work in your Spheres of Life. The growth of the Soul is important at all times, and your Souls, like the trees, and the flowers, and all growing things upon the Earth, must have the right conditions before they can come to perfection. You ask "What is necessary for the growth of the Soul"?

The first step is the real knowledge of the self, and having the strength to set aside all the imaginings and wishings of the physical mind. Then, ruthlessly cutting out of your life, all that creates the conditions of thought and action that you know stand in the way of your progression. This means, that you find yourself in what you call a "lonely" condition. You cannot enter with the same pleasure into what has, before, secured for you all you needed. You try to force yourself back into the old ways and then begins that war between the progressing and the progressed Soul Forces and the physical self.

How hard, how lonely, how sad and depressing your little self finds that Way! Here is your first testing—here is where you come to what you call "LONELINESS"—but it is really the first and most important step to the *finding* of the Self.

It is no good now to rely upon the physical things of life to help you out of these conditions. You must turn within, to where your TRUE STRENGTH lies. Put yourself into the Hands of God, flood your *Being* with the Infinite Peace of His Love. Set your mind firmly and sternly in what you are truly seeking, to achieve, in your REAL SELF—your REAL PURPOSE of LIFE and *then* you will come to the Light you seek.

The Spiritual Forces cannot and must not interfere with your Free will, but they *can* and *do* bring to you countless opportunities for using that Freewill in the way that will lead you to the Path. How unconscious are you of their Presence when you go down into the depths of self-pity and self-love, yet they stand by you, ever ready to strengthen and to help you to seek and to find that which is of God. So often you will not open yourselves to receive that help! You turn instead to the problems that beset you and your minds become like a pool that is always being stirred—deeper and deeper you go until at last comes that sad saying "It's no use"! "I don't seem to be able to get any help"! My Chelas! those are terrible words and sounds to release in the ethers of your world. You not only add to your own burden, but you add to the burden of others in like condition and you deny the Truth of Him who said "I will not leave thee comfortless". To be ever confident of the constant help of the Loving Father, to know that you will not be turned aside, but that at all times and in all conditions you stand in His Presence, is your sure and certain help. This you all know, but will not always allow yourselves to remember.

When you plant a seed or root in the Earth, you prepare the conditions of the soil. You do not then turn aside and leave it, you watch, you tend, you give it all you feel it needs to help it in its upward way and you are sure that into the soil God will give the Elements necessary for its progress. Likewise, you watch plants, trees, and flowers that grow without care which man can give them, but they are never away from the care which God gives them.

When you come to the Realisation, that the power of developing your own Soul to reach Perfection lies in your own Will Power, you have taken your first steps towards preparing the Soul for its growth, but that is not enough.

You too, give to them constantly through the emanations of your Soul, the food necessary for growth and progression in all Kingdoms of Life, vegetable, mineral, animal and human alike, so that quite unconsciously you are helping in the growth of all Evolution.

If you remember the Teachings of the Master Jesus, you will know that He constantly spoke of growth in all its forms.

When He sought to teach those who listened how best to live, He pointed to the way of Life in the other Kingdoms around them —the birds, the sheep, the hills, the rivers, the seas, the flowers, the trees and the stones. Always did He show the Hand of God in all forms of Life, yet man, whose body is composed of those very elements, does not think of the continual watching and tending them. Nevertheless, the Father-Mother of All Life know the needs of all He has created, and is ready always through His Almighty Force to supply those needs. Do *not* rely so much upon your physical learning or knowledge—that is of the human mind. The great Spirit has given you that Power which we call for you *Intuition* and if you will earnestly and with His Help, try to learn how to know and use that Power in your lives, there is no Force in life, yours or any others, than can overcome you. The Soul depends on your active Force for its growth, not that force which is supplied by the physical mind, but that Force which comes from the Inner Being which is not concerned with your life in its physical form only, but with your life in all its aspects, or forms and forces.

That is what so often is forgotten. Form is merely an outward manifestation. The Force within Form supplies the power necessary for growth spiritually.

If deeper thought were given to this truth so reliance on physical things would diminish in earthly living. Inner Consciousness would be used and clear, Spiritual Seeing and understanding which is limitless would develop.

What do you ask for in your Developing Classes? Do you come to develop Psychic Gifts, or do you remember that as you learn to know more of the Inner Self, the Consciousness of your Being, the Psychic Forces, will blend into the Spiritual and develop with them? Do you try to let the thought of others pass from your mind and become relaxed and stilled in all parts of your physical self? That must be the first step in your Spiritual Development—to learn to "go apart"—not just when you are alone, or in prepared conditions and surroundings, but when you are with others, and all the bustle of the world is around you.

We find so many of you still demand prepared conditions for your Spiritual Advancement, yet, as Christians, you say "you would walk the Master's Way". Well! He walked in the World and brought His Spirituality into all He did in the World. He still does so, through each one of you, when you give Him the opportunity for it. It was not always what He said [though people make that very important today] and that was an important part of His Work but He lived His Teachings. Those around Him saw the proof of all He taught.

Today, in your world people fear Truth. They fear to face it in their own living and in the lives of others. How then, if fear walks with you on your way, can you expect to know and love the Blessed Father of All?

You must transmute Fear by using and living Love, for that, as He truly said, will "Cast out Fear".

The growth and progression of the Soul is a process of Transmutation. If you find that a tree or a plant is not producing its leaves and flowers as it should, and you wish it to produce well, you get to work to find out why it does not thrive. You search for and try every means to help its growth and that is what you need to do in your own lives. Know that your growth is dependent on what you are taking into your life. Make sure that you feed your Soul—the unprogressed part—with the Power of the Spirit and then it will grow upwards towards the Light and all your days will be filled with His Love.

As you go upon your Way of Life, the outflowing of that Love will also feed others, through all the parts of the Mind, and the

Body, which are the gifts of God to you. Then will you be AT ONE (ALL ONE—alone) with Him.

O Great Spirit, who alone can create the Power of Life, bless the seeking ones, stretch forth Thy Hand to give them of Thy Help and Thy Wisdom that they may come to the recognition of their helplessness without Thy Loving Care—and in that knowing—they will come to Thee and receive Thy Blessing and Thy Eternal Peace. Amen.

CHAPTER 3

THE CYCLE OF NECESSITY

"I am a part of all that I have met"! These words of a great poet, how true they are, but I wonder very much if we ever dwell or think of these any more than superficially?

It is a gigantic thought to think that we are all a part of those whom we have met and still do meet, and are meeting! This could also give to us both pleasant and unpleasant thoughts and feelings, but surely, when we think of the process of Evolution, we realise that all at some time or another pass through most revolting stages of living! When we recognise them as such, we know that we must either have experienced or still must experience these stages, it causes us greatly to think, when we see faults in another. How can we recognise something in others, if we have not experienced, or are experiencing it ourselves? One cannot recognise anything that one hasn't known! This should teach us a measure of tolerance and understanding, and help us to become deeply humble in our thinking and treatment of others.

If we are a part of all that we have met, and if, as we believe, we have, and are passing through, or have already passed through these varying experiences of poverty (mind and body), of wealth, of insecurity, and of all the other vices or virtues that one could name, and we know and recognise these, then we must at some time or another, have experienced them, or may even still be experiencing them, how tolerant we should be of others!

"First cast out the mote that is within thine own eye" is an excellent maxim, but let us remember also, that this does not imply "softness" in the dealing with these things. To "Know Thyself" was one of the first teachings of the Master Jesus, and surely it is true that we cannot know others, until we first know and recognise ourselves. We must recognise not just the superficial man, that hides the truth of what he is, behind a façade for others to admire, but the real ego, his soul, at which he does not care to gaze, because it becomes too painful.

Accordingly, the Truth is pushed away and unaccepted, and the living in a state of deception to oneself continues. Later perhaps, more courage is gained and the not too pretty picture is taken out again and looked at, and may be partly accepted. NOT until each one has the courage of the God Force to see himself as he really is, and not as he wishes others to think he is, will any progress be made. No! this is not an easy accomplishment, but one which is a necessity if the soul within is to develop and grow and if the desire to help others is real and lasting. When man "knows himself" he knows, also, every other man—his weakness and his strength. NOT until he himself knows how to use the Strength of God, to transform the ugliness that he sees within himself, can he point the way for others in truth and humility. When this point is reached, then the strength of purpose, the power of God, will pour upon him to help him in his hour of Gethsemane, in his wanderings in the wilderness, in his own crucifixion upon the Cross of Suffering, to realise the Cross of Service. It will help him to an acceptance of his better self, in surrender to all that is good, uplifting and creative. He will then know the Peace that passes all understanding, for he has a realisation of the Truth, a glimpse of Reality, and a goal to reach that is not beyond his capabilities. In other words, he will then know the Power of God operating within and around him. Having thus passed through the "fires" as it were, he is then in a position to "*know*" and to "*be*" and to *help others* as he helped himself. He now stands in command of himself, with a wide and varied vista before him, He knows and realises his true strength, and is ready to place his feet upon a Path that is beset with trials and tests that get more subtle as he treads the Way, but every step will lead him steadily towards his goal, and to the Light of Lights.

Let us not think for one moment that such an achievement is easy to attain, or that we can reach it by any dominant physical quality. Just as in acquiring knowledge to fit oneself to take a place in the physical world, so one must work and strive continuously to attain the things of the Spirit.

To tenaciously cling to all that is taught, to be constantly on the alert to watch for pitfalls in one's evolution, and to blend at all times the physical living with the perception of the Spirit, is not easy. After all, if you do not make mistakes how are you to learn? I would therefore emphasise the fact, that to make mistakes is the only sure method of experiencing the right or wrong way, what is unacceptable is the constant making of the same error, and many times to an even worse degree.

"A Teacher can but point the Way" is true, for He cannot live the life for you. You must put into constant practice that which is shown to you, and you must use your own Freewill at all times, make your own decisions and choose for yourselves. He cannot and will not interfere with your Freewill, which is God's great gift to mankind. Neither will He break what is a Spiritual Law!

People blame God for their misfortunes—they say "Why does God allow it?" or perhaps "What have I done to deserve this?" They must always have someone or something to blame, but many times, if they really stopped to think, they would find that they themselves are responsible for their misfortunes and not God at all!

Mankind brings suffering upon himself so often and he fails to see the reason, or does not wish to find it, because it is so much easier to blame God. If he has the courage to face himself and look for the cause of the trouble, he will be a better and a stronger person for having done so, because then, and only then, can he set to work to rectify that which is wrong within himself. That, surely, is the purpose of living! To create perfection, to right that which has gone wrong, to grow each day in the strength of God, and to realise the purpose of this sojourn in the world to become more versed in the ways of the Spirit and of God, each day you live.

Revelation is a wonderful thing! Only by this can we succeed, and truly find the courage to live and realise His Love for each one of us. This is not easy, but very worthwhile.

No one can let us use his eyes. We must use our own, to see the self, to extricate ourselves from the selfish, possessive ego, and become the selfless, ever-growing ego of the Higher Self.

And so we live this Earth life, or the Cycle of Necessity, as we call it, which is really the life of a Soul upon any plane to which it goes. There it may learn the lessons of living and using these lessons, bring the Higher Self to assist in bringing his Soul Forces into Harmony with all that is pure, and all that is God-like. Here, upon the Earth Plane, are many opportunities of finding the way to bring personality (which is physical) into a purer blending with Individuality which is the true expression of the Higher Self (the Spiritual Self). Before this can be accomplished we must seek to know and use the full control of the mind. It would be of no use to seek the highest in the expression of our lives, until we know how to attain it.

People speak of the "Silence of the Soul" but not always do they realise what they mean by that, nor how best to use it.

Silence means, for you, the ceasing of physical sound, but that is not what is meant by silence esoterically. Silence here, is the stilling or lessening of sound in our own minds, irrespective of what is going on around us. It is the raising of the vibratory force of our own lesser thoughts, until they can blend into perfect attunement with the Higher Self, when thought becomes Consciousness.

This is not such a difficult thing as it sounds. It appears difficult, because we think of it in a physical way, yet all around us, in the world, it is being demonstrated. Although we cannot see them, cannot hear them, in the silence there are sounds, but until we become attuned to them by physical mechanism we are not sure that they are there! I refer, of course, to wireless, and television. People who lived here hundreds of years ago would not have believed them possible, just as we, in our age, cannot believe what in days to come will be an accepted fact by the people of that day. This is due to the limitation with which we bind ourselves. We insist on measuring our capabilities, by what we say, or know we are able and fitted to do, yet how often do we come to some phase or experience in our lives which we said we could not go through and yet we have done so! This is why we call this part of our Spiritual and Soul Life a "Cycle of Necessity".

It is necessary for the advancement of the Soul, to experience conditions where it may have the opportunities of finding its own power to deal with them in such a way that progression from Personality to Individuality can rapidly be fulfilled.

Today, one of the most dreadful things that can happen to man is to develop the aura of apathy, the insistence that he cannot do this or that, the growth more and more of the evasion of responsibility and his willing acceptance of others doing for him what he should be doing for himself, in order to fulfill his purpose here. "That is not my work"—how often do you hear that said? How often do you say it? Do you realise in these words the limitation of life and living? It may be a task someone else should do. Are you quite sure always, that it may not be an opportunity for you to help another Soul, not by depriving the soul of its opportunity, but by showing how the task could be done, blending into selflessness your own actions. Here of course, you must use discrimination. It might well be, that in doing the work someone else should do, you would not really be helping them. This is where you should not rely upon your physical thoughts and inclinations but discern by your Intuition what is the Truth and how you should act. Life is full of such opportunities. You overlook the little ways of testing your own powers and fail to use the power of Discernment or what is better known as Perception. You seek the bigger and more spectacular ways, but remember the Teaching that "unless ye be perfect in the little things, ye cannot be perfect in the greater"!

How good it would be, if we put into practice more often in our daily life, the small kindnesses that are so often kept for people outside our own family. The desire to create an impression of our own goodness or cleverness, or capability, upon those with whom we come into contact, with no thought whatever of the effect upon the evolution of the Self, or upon the world, of which we are a part, and what is most important of all, the responsibility to God, who gave us the power to live, gave us life which is His gift and which we so often treat as belonging to us alone.

Why do we not bring Spiritual Aspirations into constant action of our everyday lives? Is it not because we draw a dividing line between the physical and the spiritual? This, in spite of the fact that we have been taught that the physical self cannot live by "Bread alone", but must draw upon a Spiritual source and strength for everything it wants to do. Why then, do we not train ourselves to think of spiritual actions in our physical deeds until it becomes quite effortless to do so? The whole physical training of our lives teaches the power of the self; but those who are Chelas, or students of the Esoteric Teachings, know that self is dependent on the power of the Higher Self. The Self—Mind and Body—has limitation but the true Self—the blending of the Higher with the Highest, has no limitations whatever.

Our senses, feelings, and emotions are all the outlets of the physical self. So long as we depend on the mind force to control them, we shall not travel very far, but continue to travel in a circle, always returning to the same point. Only one Power can help us to break free, the Power of our own Being—of which perception is a part. To "perceive" is far more than just to see, for to perceive is a spiritual vibration and has a wiser, deeper meaning.

When we truly use Perception, we do not remain on the outside, but go right to the heart of the matter. We do not examine the *effect,* we seek and find the *cause* and in that, we take the first steps towards changing it. Often, the cause is unpleasant to us and we turn away. Surely the moment that the revelation and realisation of wrong comes to us, the Individuality should come into action and compel the Personality to submit to the Higher Purpose! When the help, for which we ask, is available, so many turn away and refuse to use it, because it is not what the mind has conceived as being the *necessary* help.

Spiritual Aspiration should be active in all our lives, in thought, and in our deeds. To aspire spiritually is not a physical or a mental action, any more than prayer is a form of words. Prayer is an utterance from the Soul, put sometimes into words, but more often, when sincere, not even a conscious thought—just a "knowing" within. That, as we well know, does not need to be put into the sounds of earth to reach the Master of All! Spiritual Aspiration will become a part of our life, when we have given up, or should I say, blended all our desires, hopes and wishes into the actions of our lives. We do not have to think of what our Spirit is seeking. We know that it is ever seeking a fuller blending with the God Force of all Life, and this can only be attained by using the Power of God in the *smallest* degrees of living.

To set apart a time for communion with God is not necessary, if that whole action of living is already that Communion. We cannot set God apart from our lives at any given place or time. That is limitation again—the limitation of Mind and Body.

Make a conscious awareness of the God Force in every word you speak, every deed, and your struggles are over. Acceptance is a blending of life and action, so how can we tell of what we are capable until we test ourselves and find out.

Many find it difficult to be really natural and constantly struggle to conform to the standards of the world which have been set down. In doing so, they deliberately hold back their own growth.

Attainment can only come by compelling the conditions of, and in our lives, to yield up to us their fullest opportunities. We watch opportunity come, but instead of measuring the worth of what has come and using it for greater opportunities for getting deeper into the Innermost Self, grasping the weakness of the Soul, and bringing it for Transmutation into strength, this opportunity is looked at purely from the physical aspect, we use it, or turn aside from it because of our worldly-minded reaction to it. Look at problems, not from the physical aspect only, but try to see in these problems opportunities for silent seeking and for the finding of the "True Self". To learn how to *"go apart"* to be conscious of discerning that which will make you "God Conscious without any physical thinking".

We are all dependent, one upon the other! Be free of others and use the freedom as the Beloved Master taught His Followers to use it! By using *Perception* instead of physical thinking and understanding, we can be of far greater service to those in the world here and in the Worlds beyond, who are in need of help. This will be an unconscious action, not done in thought, but by the Spirit.

All things that *"happen"* in our lives are not mere happenings. They are the effects of some *Cause* in the Soul Life.

A change of environment does not just mean something that gives us an opportunity of living in a different way. If we are truly seeking a Way of Attainment, we shall see, in that change, an answer to the cry of the Soul-self, a way, by which we receive something that will help us to find and truly know the Self, the Higher Self, that is seeking fulfilment in this "Cycle of Necessity" —a good name for the Earth life, which is today, restless, self seeking, interdependent, and grasping. Why? Are we not all afraid that we shall not get what the desire self is seeking? Yet, by using these measures, the possibility of true attainment will slip away! Take a little of your much valued "time" to think of these things. Let problems and difficulties slip away from thought, into silence, the Silence of your Innermost Being. You will know and feel, by

Perception, the purpose of what has come to you, and why things do not work out as you expect.

Grasp and use these opportunities, for the growth and development of the Soul Forces, so that, in company with All-Love and Wisdom, you will be at one with your Purpose of Life, in the Cycle of Necessity, and use the circumstances for growth and for giving Spiritual counsel and guidance to others. Do not say, "I am not fit to do this"! If you feel that, it is for you to make yourself fit, and until you begin to try to help others, you cannot possibly know how much you *can* do, nor in what way it can be done!

May God's Blessing be in your thoughts and deeds, and may He Light your Way through the Cycle of Necessity, so that you, taking His Gifts, turn darkness into light, suffering into Joy, or give, in your way of Living and Sounding in the Silence, of His Peace and His Love.

CHAPTER 4

ACCEPTANCE

You can see, from the previous chapters, that man, having a lower self, or a part of himself, that needs to be helped, that there are many thousands of souls upon the earth who are finding great difficulty in the transmutation of that self, i.e. the lower self. The greatest difficulty being that the obstacles are found, not in the big things of life, but in the many small ways that come to you in the daily living of your lives, and where you have the opportunity of exercising your Free Will, or submitting yourself to the desire of your Minds and Bodies.

The first and most important act in all your daily living is to find *"Acceptance"* and use it. I do not mean acceptance in its earthly meaning, for if you use it, in that sense, you will not be "enduring" but *submitting.* If you think of this, calling on the Higher or Spiritual Self to help, you will find a great difference here. *"Acceptance"* in its Esoteric or Spiritual sense means the blending of your Force of Will, not the physical will-power, but the True Force—into whatever conditions you are trying to clear.

There is a part of your lives that calls for you to conform to rules and regulations, or to the wishes of those from whom you receive payment for service rendered, but you will have to conform to their ruling. That does not mean that you accept them as being the right thing to do or the *right* way to act. The very fact that you do *"accept"* these will bring into all your thoughts and actions in respect of those duties the Forces of the Spirit, which, quite unconsciously to you, will go on working through you in those conditions.

The important thing is, that you do not seek reward, nor even recognition for any service given, whether Spiritual or Physical. If you *do* find yourselves seeking tangible results, then you will know quite clearly that you are *NOT* seeking Spiritually.

In the fulfilling of the Law, i.e. the Law of Love—there are seven aspects. One of these aspects is the *Law of Balance*—another, the *Law of Compensation,* and in your quiet moments when you do, or should do, make an adjustment of your three planes of consciousness, you will surely find that Balance is badly needed.

In the lives of people today, there is a decided tendency to take up one particular line of thought or action, and to put away everything that will not fall into place with that. You, in your mental struggles make insuperable barriers in trying "to be", but if you measure everything by your physical standards of measurement, omitting all that is of the Spiritual Self, you will never reach any worthwhile conclusion. You have to concentrate less on the lower self, and remember that you are also a Spiritual Self, *now,* at this particular moment. No good saying, as you will, "this makes me feel an important person". If it does, then it proves that you are still dwelling in the lower self and that all you have done is to magnify its proportion.

This world will go on just the same as it is now, even if you are suddenly transported from flesh to spirit! Your physical absence may cause a gap, perhaps sorrow, and a blank in the lives of others, but life will go on, and that alone should bring home to you of how little is the importance of the self, in the world plan, but you know that you are a part of a greater plan—the Plan of Evolution—*That* cannot go on without any one of you, since you are all necessary to the perfecting of that plan, because you all help to maintain the Balance.

Pride of Self is one of the greatest enemies of Evolution, and if you look at the state of the world today you will find *that* quality (pride of self) is at the root of the unrest and disquiet that has spread, and is still spreading, in your world. You cannot separate yourselves from all the world, and many will, perhaps, find that hard to accept, and still harder to remember that all the world is affected by the Vibrations of your lives, or any simple action in your lives is a stupendous thought, but so is the thought of God—yet you believe in God, and that the Vibratory Force of God is in your lives. Why then if you acknowledge that it is by the vibrating of God's Forces in and through you, that you go on living, can you not acknowledge that Force mingling with all you make from it, and that it flows forth from you too?

There is no half-way in Truth, as many would like to think. There is really no half-way in Reality at all. There is Positive and Negative. Reason as you will with your physical minds, you cannot alter Truth. It is very easy to take up an attitude of Mind in the physical life, but it is not so easy a matter to alter it. To the many who have this difficulty I would say, try first, to reach a clear perspective of your self, and build, in its place, a picture of yourself as a Blending of Purity and Impurity, each struggling to be uppermost, then set to work with a positive vibration to change yourself. Do not say "I have tried and failed". Failing is only a matter of trying in the wrong way. Remember, if you do not make mistakes, you cannot possibly learn.

Remember too, the words of Jesus, the Christos, "I am the Way". It is only by following this Way that you can change yourselves. Are you pleased or satisfied with your way of thinking and living? No? Why not? What is wrong? Do I hear you say "It seems as though everything in my life is wrong"? That cannot possibly be! Do you realise that?! You cannot take the God-Force out of your lives, or you would cease to live physically. If you have ever watched Death, you know, quite clearly, that, at that change, something passes from the physical Mind and Body, so that they no longer function. What is it that passes? The God-Force or Spirit!

Very well, you cannot just store it up in you, for you are constantly in the act of receiving and giving, every moment of your lives. Therefore, there *is* something in you, that is *not* wrong. You plunge yourselves into darkness when you refuse to acknowledge and accept the Power of God in you, just as you plunge a room into darkness when you turn off the light, or you switch off a machine, but that does not mean that you have caused that power to cease from functioning. It is still there waiting to be used, and when you, too, make the effort to release into action your Spiritual Force, then the others will again be filled with light or sound. This is what happens in your lives. You take a trend of thought or action and cut off everything you do not wish to obtrude in that course; but the power to obtrude is still there and according to your acceptance of your own Spiritual—Physical sources of living, so you can use, or not use the Force or Power that will help you towards the Evolution of your Soul. You must recognise and accept the Truth, that there are many ways of expressing yourselves. Still more important, you have the right to choose your way, for you alone are held responsible in the Higher Life for what you have made of yourselves. You cannot forcibly alter the lives of other people. If you believe that you can, then you deny Freewill, and if you deny Freewill, then you deny God; that, I am sure, you will not find easy to do, as every minute you live and breathe and move is a proof of the Power of God within. You have all, at some time or another, come into contact with children who were suffering from "growing pains"! A good many people also suffer from "growing pains" of the Soul!

The abysmal darkness into which many plunge themselves, and in which they take such a gloomy view of themselves, should really bring a warm glow to the heart, for it is a clear indication that the Spiritual Self has given a greater power to the growing Soul. The "growing" or the evolving Soul is fighting hard, to help the physical mind to come to the point of "Acceptance". This should be a matter for rejoicing and not for saying "I can't believe", "I can't understand", "I can't change myself". The very fact that you think this, ought to be a clear proof that mentally you are resisting the "growing pains". You cause yourselves a great deal of unnecessary suffering and mental distress, which invariably causes a loss of Balance, then you take a darkened viewpoint of your own life into action, and probably other people's actions too. You assign all sorts of distorted reasons to things which have quite a simple explanation.

This is the time to turn on the Light of God, and the Light of Truth to those distorted thoughts and accept the Truth, that in you is God. There is no need to go out to find God, whatever you may think of yourselves, or whatever others may think of you. God is within you and around you, at all times, this Force passing through you night and day and nothing you can do will ever stop that flow. All you can do, is to refuse to use it as it should be used, but that flow is the proof of Love that is pure and selfless. Nothing can alter that Love. It will still continue to serve you. This is Truth—

God is giving you His Service, every moment of your lives, and nothing can ever change it.

All True Servers need to learn this and so make themselves determined to prove worthier to receive and accept that priceless gift of Love.

You all know how you feel when someone hurts you. You may have a strong desire to retaliate, to hurt, in return. It may be done secretly in the Mental Planes, by which that force will be directed to you through thought, but God's Servers will never choose either course. From them should continue to flow a steady stream of pure, desireless love, that will never cease to flow, and will never be diverted from its course by anything that can be said or done.

When you are offered a gift, you do not accept it with hands that are already filled. You first empty them, so that you may fully receive the gift. That is what God asks of us—to empty ourselves, so that He may give of His Love and His Force, but He will never ask for your acceptance. He does not seek to compel you to take them. When you say you cannot feel the Presence of God, and His Vibration of Love, surely the reason is that you are "out of Balance" and you allow desire of self, or of others, or the material things of life to overcrowd and outweigh the desire of your Evolving Soul.

If you would but accept the great gift of Love and Wisdom and put it into action in your daily living, the whole trend of your thought and action would alter. It cannot be otherwise; but do not expect this to take place in a moment of time, as a miracle. First of all, you must remove bit by bit, those thoughts and actions that prevent you from finding True Balance. When this is done, the Law of Compensation will come into being in your lives. You will begin to find a more abiding sense of peace than anything Earth can give, you will find that in the acceptance of your at-one-ness with this great Divine Love, darkness cannot overpower you. The material things of this life cannot dismay you, and your whole outlook in Life will be clearer, and of that wider vision, that is of the Spirit. The growth will go on and possibly the "growing pains" too, for adjustment is a painful process; but you will find added strength to bear whatever comes to you. No, this is not an easy or very simple way to travel, but when you have the true acceptance in your lives, you will not rebel, you will not question, you will not stir up discontent within, but come in calmness and strength to the struggle of life as the Christ showed could be done. Never forget the words "What I have done, all men may do". You may not be called upon to suffer as He did, but you will be tried and tested.

You expect to be tested in your earthy life, for only by that "testing" are you worthy to be offered something. Why is it that you expect the Gifts of the Spirit to be given to you to use without even proving that you are worthy of bearing them? In the small ways of life these tests will come, because they are always harder to bear. "No man cometh unto the Father but by me" said the Christos, while in the Earth. Join that to His Words "I am the Truth and the Way" and you will find the foundation for True Spiritual growth.

Refuse to take refuge in deceit, untruth and dishonesty in however small the way! Be resolute, for that is more important than anything in your lives. Only you yourselves will have to account for your actions, but you alone are responsible for the vibrations you release in your day to day living. Are they good and positive? Or not good? Within your *hearts* and not your minds, you know the answer for your heart is the Centre of your Being, and there truth lies for you to see and use.

May he who is all Love, shed His Light upon your Path, may His Strength be ever in and around you and may He in His Loving Mercy, bless you in your Acceptance of His Love and grant you His Peace upon your Way.

Chapter 5

THE FULFILLING OF THE LAW

There have been many times and there are still, when the cries from you for Peace are, from your hearts, raised to God.

Many are the ways that are sought for attainment, many are the ideals, and ideas which you set forth, but many have been taught and know within, the only way to attain Peace.

To stir the Spirit within, the Wisdom that is there, to bring forth through the consciousness of your own Being, those Forces, which, if you will but permit them to work through you, will truly bring that for which you so often pray—the Will of the Great All-Father to be close in the Earthly Place of Existence.

The Fulfilling of the Laws—the using of Love—but you must not be mistaken in the understanding of that word. You must not allow yourselves to be satisfied with what often is, but a reflection of Love, that which arises in the human mind, which comes forth in expression in the human body, and in the human ways of living. Do not feel satisfied within yourselves, that when you feel in the consciousness of earthly life, the outgoing, or outpouring of that which you call Love, that you have attained to the Wisdom that *is* Love.

The Law which is Love, has many aspects. The main aspects are seven in number, and are ever functioning in your lives. You must come to the understanding of these aspects, that one is the complement of the other, and each is a part of the whole, and that they must work within if you are to attain the Peace within that you so much seek. The Aspects of the Law are—Order, Compensation, the Law of Karma, or cause and effect, Vibration,

Balance, Cycles and Polarity—and there we have the true Divine Law of Love operating in each of these aspects, in perfect harmony in all conditions of life.

God has given Man dominion over the different Kingdoms of the Earth. The lower kingdoms you call them, and lower they may be, but only in the sense of not being able to express the Divine Consciousness—that Man has which is of the Higher Order of Life, and yet, so often in these Planes of Existence you can see the working of that Divine Consciousness in the Perfection of their giving Forth.

Let us dwell briefly upon these aspects of Love of which I have spoken.

All things in life are ordered and when you come to the Realisation of that, when you allow yourselves to believe—mark well that phrase—when you *allow* yourselves to believe—that is to say consciously upon the physical brain matter in the Wisdom that lies in the Spirit, you realise that nothing can happen by chance, nothing by accident. There is a purpose in all manifestations of Life, and if there is purpose there is *ORDER*. In the World of Spirit there is no confusion. It matters not what happens in this realm, all is still in perfect order. You do not find a losing of the senses, and such rushing hither and thither. You will not find either the purposeless seeking that we find among the races of the Earthly Plane, because in the World of Spirit you have passed beyond the confines of these things we ourselves have created, in order to limit our Being—we become at one—with the Divine Purpose, and so will become part of that Harmony and having done so, our life becomes ORDERED.

When you realise this, and find in your lives barriers and difficulties, when you see obstacles which you feel cannot be overcome if then you would remember that ORDER is part of the Divine Law—that ORDER is an aspect of Love, you will then realise that there must be a Force in actual Life that necessitates the creation of those conditions. You cannot be in any condition of life where there is no purpose. Many say "Why must we suffer?" Surely you suffer because suffering is but the negative aspect of which the positive aspect is Love. Suffering is the distortion of Love and brought about, not by the Will of God, but out of the Divine Wisdom of God, that knew that all things had been distorted and must find their way out of the distortion and become again in perfect Harmony, Order and Compensation—which is a part of Order. No matter what your lives may be, no matter what their sphere or condition, there will always be the *Law of Compensation.*

If you look at disorders in your lives, you must realise that when you set them in order, you are using Divine Wisdom, for the Wisdom of the physical manifestation of Love must if necessary be limited to form. The Divine Wisdom is Force and when you apply that Wisdom-Force to any condition in your lives, you find instantly the Law of Compensation at work, and where there has been disorder, you will find in it the compensating force of Harmony the moment you begin to put it right, for then and only then there will be the actual setting into motion of that Force. Only then will you begin to realise why the disorder occurred, and that it was not caused by something *outside* yourselves, but because of lack of order within and here it is you come to the Law of Cause and Effect or Karma.

Order, Compensation and Karma—three aspects, yet as three must ever be, three in one—for you cannot separate them. You will find the Law of Cause and Effect, or Karma must always work in the Laws of Order, and the Laws of Compensation. Karma is *not* a law of Retribution, nor of reward. It is the Law of Cause and Effect, and therefore whatever is in your lives, you can always find the cause—and I do ask you when looking for a cause of disorder, inharmony, hardship and suffering, look first within—and then without, for you cannot and will not find order in yourselves until you have tried to find your shortcomings.

Whatever the conditions of your lives may be, and although it may seem to you as forced upon you by others, you can rest assured, that if you are affected in any way, then it is because in the Soul, there is a part of it awaiting transmutation and those conditions are the opportunities for that transmutation to take place. Cause and Effect must be worked out. It is a Divine Law and as a Divine Law is Perfect Love. He who gave you life, who gave life to all, has that Wisdom that knows, that only in the True understanding of the Creative Force, will you realise what Cause and Effect really mean. If therefore, you create a cause, you will see its effect and know that you are the creator of such, and that you must use Divine Consciousness in all your physical and soul expressions to the manifestation of life in its true order. If you do do so, the Law of Compensation will help you to adjust the effect of whatever was the cause. How often do you say "We are not responsible" for conditions that are occurring "I have led my life peacefully" and "sought to be of service to mankind". "I have tried to do my best, and never sought to harm anyone." Search long and deep within, and when you do so, can you say you are absolutely blameless? Are you sure that no thought has arisen in your Mental Body that has gone out into the ethers of the Planes of Life, and there has caused unharmony and discord? If it has then you have added one more vibration to the force of destruction—against the Force of Compensation to the Divine Law and its fulfilment. Order, Compensation, Karma—three and there standing in the centre, you come to *Vibration* which is the Force of Life, the Breath of Eternal Motion. I emphasise—The *Breath of Eternal Motion.* That is what Vibration is in your lives. There is no stillness, there is perpetual motion in all forms of life. That is again the Law of Love—onwards, or backwards—for nothing ever remains static.

You have the Divine Consciousness with which you can perfect the rate of Vibration. All things within these Planes of Life are vibrating, nothing is still. It is for you, to whom the Great Spirit has given dominion to use your Force of Vibration, which emanates from the Divine Force of Love, to see that all around you is being acted upon by the perfect vibration of your lives.

Why are you so disturbed by outer happenings? Why is it that you build a fabric which seems fair and strong to you? Suddenly, a condition enters your lives and the whole world seems to change—you feel peace and harmony flowing around you—and then perchance a day comes when a word may be spoken, an action done and the whole fabric is destroyed, the peace and harmony gone. You search wildly in many such conditions and ask "What is the cause of this?" By being so distressed and disturbed you only add to the confusion. Never can you attain peace if you have not peace within yourselves and the first law to yourselves must be that you strive to keep the perfect vibration of your own Being. How can you attain it? Only on the understanding of that which is your True Self—the Perfect Triune—

Spirit, Soul and Body—each functioning separately and yet as one! Spirit permeating through all the Forces of your lives, your Soul always desiring to go on its Way—or maybe to go back—even if it has chosen this way of life that it may satisfy a part of itself that seeks to go back upon the Path, there must be another part of the Soul that is evolved beyond that desire. If this part of the Soul is strong enough it could send out the Vibratory Force of its own Spiritual Being into your life, with all the fulness of Force, Order and Compensation. Then Karma will be set in action and they will be drawn into the perfect Vibration of your Life. You will then find that whatever outer happenings there may be, nothing can disturb the inward calm.

Next comes *Balance*—for when you have used the true Vibration of your own Spiritual Being, when the Breath of Eternal Motion is working in strength and force, then you find Balance.

"Know Thyself" He said, when He walked the Plane of Earth. "Know thyself that thou mayest attain to the Way of Attainment." You cannot come to the Way of Attainment until you know Balance which is a matter of understanding the Power that is within you—the Breath of God it is sometimes called. What is the Breath of God? Surely the manifestation of the Divine within yourselves brought into Being and expressed through the physical living that alone can bring True Balance.

The Earth is still seeking Balance. The Water Carrier has gone forth, the Water of Life is being brought to the Earth that it may water the soil and make it grow fertile. The Earth is trying today to attain Balance, but until Man recognises that Balance cannot be found by attainment of earthly things, he will not come to the True Balance of his own Being.

Balance can only be brought about by using Vibratory Force in such a way, that Wisdom, not only understanding, but *Wisdom* is applied to all physical living. You must apply the wisdom of the Spirit to all ways of living and cease to be bound and held by things around you.

You say you must abide by the laws of physical living. How much do you abide by them and why? Is it not because those laws made by man are for the so called safety of man? God too has given you laws—but He does not compel you to obey them.

He gives you the right to use the power to say "I will", or "will not" —Freewill—the greatest gift of God to mankind. If you ask for Peace in your lives then you must be prepared not to let the physical ways of life dominate you and throw you completely out of balance by your ways of living. If you do you cannot vibrate the True Force of Wisdom and Love into the Earth.

Discord and unharmony alone can be the result of the negative aspect of Love, which is often in its physical manifestation, love of wealth, love of power, love of self, love of those around you. By no means are any of these to be decried and condemned, for they are but the outward physical manifestations, but by the same token you have to learn the Balance of these things and know that to be possessed by them or these loves is putting yourselves out of Balance and denying your Spiritual Self the right to exist in the physical aspect of your lives.

The aspects of Love manifest in Cycles. Look back through the history of the world and see that all manifestations of Force work in Cycles. It works in a perfect circle, is sent out, and returns and it is a Law of Love that you can watch it in your own lives if you choose to do so. You cry out "Why is this? Why is that?" Search well within, and so often you will find the answer there. You will find that what you are looking at now is not the *Cause,* but the *Effect* and if you trace back along the path of Effect, you will surely come to the Cause. You will also find that confusion and the conditions that disorder your lives, have been caused by the distortion of the Force of Balance.

Many times, the gifts which God has bestowed upon mankind have been seen and also recognised, and perchance he has sought the beauty of those gifts and then gradually a small part of the unprogressed soul has come strongly into action and in a very short time has overthrown the true desire for Truth and Beauty and limited its Force to form. It is all around you in the World today—vibratory force being distorted and used for the satisfaction of the senses, physical desires and only until that cycle has been worked through and man has, by his own living force, perfected again, that which he has distorted, can it be rectified.

And now we come to *Polarity*—a necessity in the life of all earthly kingdoms. You have a negative and a positive aspect in all forms of life. Until man truly recognises himself and stands forth in this world as Spirit, and refuses to function entirely on his own physical Plane of Life, resolving to manifest his own Spiritual Being while yet in the Earthly Body that must remain.

Positive and negative aspects of Love are ever at work—they must be so. You say, "I do not believe in Reincarnation and the coming again into the same form of life." That is for you to decide, but if you will search and follow out your own life, setting aside the limitations which the physical brain teaches you and which you have been taught by others, and come into the consciousness of your own Soul—awareness, you will find that one life is not enough in which to fulfil that law. You must have that manifestation of Being in many Planes of Existence so that you may, so to speak, experience it in all its forms, in all its ways.

Good and Evil, these are the positive and negative conditions of Love. Good, its positive form, evil its negative.

The Force of Life, which is good—or God—is all powerful, and until the human race come to the clear and divine understanding that there is no form of life that has power to overthrow it, you will not find peace within your individual life, nor in its worldly aspect on these planes. Seek for that which is distorted—look upon the negative and by your own Spiritual Vibration, bring that negative aspect into its true Polarity and bring it into the Light—Good—God. You love one another, but only in varying degrees. You say you give all your love to someone or something—foolish words these are for all the Love you have to give, all the Love you have given to you is Love itself. It has no beginning and no ending, for it is Eternal, it is the fulfilling of the Law, and the Law is Love.

Therefore, if you would seek to attain peace, strive you must, in the daily living of your lives down to the smallest, the most minute detail, to express Love, and let all your living be a manifestation of Love—let it breathe in your breath, sound in your words, ring in your footsteps, be felt in your handclasps. Let Love be your watchword, your meat and drink, your waking and your sleeping and then you will truly be *Fulfilling the Law*.

Chapter 6

THE KINGDOM OF HEAVEN IS WITHIN

Always did the Master teach, that Heaven was here and now—not a state that you would travel to after passing to the Higher Life, but a state into which you could enter and receive the full joy while yet upon this Earth.

Did He not say "where your treasure is, there will your heart be also"? and if God, and all that is of God, is precious to you and of greater value than friends, wealth, or possessions, then your hearts will be filled with the Peace that is of God, and that is really what we mean when we speak of "Heaven".

We know that in your World you have many kinds of tasks to perform, and you may do them very well and the praise you receive for so doing, gives you the greatest satisfaction—you are well pleased—but that is a thing that passes—is of bodily sense and is not of what the Beloved Master spoke. To Be with the Godhead in all our thoughts and desires, is to know that you blend into, and, if need be, transmute other vibrations that are of the world.

If ye truly seek the Kingdom of Heaven which is the Peace of the Christos, then all that is needed for your true progress upon the Path, will be added. You then ask "How am I to seek to find the Kingdom of Heaven?" By finding Truth, by *living* as He did in Truth. Many say they cannot do this in this world yet you also know that there are many who do, and that it is Fear which so often drives you to be untruthful and holds you back from putting right that which you know you were wrong in doing. First then, in the seeking of the Kingdom of

Heaven you must learn to overcome fear in every form in your lives, and know that you have the power to do so! Seek it, do not turn away from it and do not use Fear, for that only holds back Progress on the Way. Seek earnestly and with Truth in your own "Being" and you will not shrink from it when you meet it, no matter what form it takes—and it has many forms as you know.

Be not afraid to confess your faults, and your weaknesses to yourself. Heed not the praise or blame of your fellow men. They cannot truly judge your reasons, or your actions, and if your lives are to be ruled by the thoughts and words of others, then truly, you are not walking in His Way, and you will never find the Kingdom.

How well He knew the weakness in each of His Disciples, their fears, their longings, their pride, their jealousies, and how earnestly He sought to help them, to bring them to the Light that He might help them in their overcoming. How often He rebuked them, and how often they were filled with resentment that He did not agree with all they desired that He should do. They were to remember often, when He had gone from this Earth world, the many obstacles they had put in their own Paths of Service and had set aside His Teachings so that they might please and satisfy the lower self, or how they had held back so much of the work they might have done, while yet He was with them, because of these physical desires.

When you see weaknesses and wrong doing in those you meet, you must hold in your minds that not all have received the True Teachings of the Christ, and that many times they do wrong, because they have no deeper knowledge of the Truth.

He taught that He was "The Way". Only by being a very part of Truth, can you ever hope to enter the Kingdom of which He taught. The Way of Truth is the Way of Crucifixion, or the death of what is false and the birth of that which is true.

Each earthly day will bring fresh opportunities each night that falls, brings a release from the hold of the Earth body and a passing to a clearer vision of the Self. If you have lived Truth, how eager will you be to pass into that pure atmosphere of Spirit, where nothing can be hidden, how glad to see with true vision what you can make right when you return to your Body.

You must not be afraid of your wrong doing, your failures, or mistakes. Seek them and let no fear dominate you—seek with the Wisdom that God has given you and "all shall be added". These are His Words and they are Truth. If you use the Vision of Spirit you cannot hold fear, for the courage of the Spirit day by day, in your ways of living will provide the Power that is constantly to be a part of your lives. A part of your lives ever, as is your work, your food, your whole life. The Power of the Christ Force will pass in and through you, and will supply to your physical being the courage and the strength to do and say what is true.

When the Master taught that it was not necessary to "take thought for the needs of the morrow," He spoke of the esoteric, or inner meaning of those words. He had even taught His followers that if they thought, spoke, and lived in Truth, no real need could ever be unsupplied with the necessary Elements to feed and strengthen it.

If you let your minds rest on His Blessed Words, you will find that in the life that is before you, that it is of little profit to gain much of what you seek in this world, if by doing so, you turn your back upon the Way of Evolution.

The world is full of unrest, of men seeking and not knowing what they seek. The Light of Christ is within each one and with Him you must help to bring Peace to mankind and if need be, by the two edged Sword of Truth. The Sword of Truth that cuts clear and clean through untruth, distrust, deceit, and all distortions of the Father—Mother of all Life. It is by the holding of Courage within that you will be able to use this Sword of the Christos and cleave the bonds that men seek to bind you with also.

Slowly the truth will come, when those who do not seek to understand His Teachings will find that they cannot live until they do. There will be no *GREAT ONE* who shall rise up and show the Way. It is for each one of you and for those who have the knowledge of the Inner Meaning of His Teachings to prove by your own ways of living, the Truth of His Words, each in their own way. Then they will know His Power, use His Courage and His Wisdom in the daily way of life.

You may live for a truth and present that which is FALSE to those whom you meet, but the hour must come when people will know you as you really are, and woe to them who have said "I would Serve Him" and yet in their everyday ways of Life, have, even as one of His Followers on Earth—denied Him.

It is Love, deep, true, and abiding that He offers. No shallow thing that is tossed hither and thither by the desires of Mind, and Body, but Love that is All Wisdom, that sees, and knows the good and the not good in every one, and yet knowing, gives of His Silent Love to guide our footsteps on the Upward Path.

CHAPTER 7

THE WAY OF ATTAINMENT

How closely is our work-a-day life woven and blended with our Spiritual Life and Spiritual Attainment?

So often you say "I have been told that I am going to do wonderful work," "I have been told I am going to do great things" and I would like you to realise that greatness only lies in the mind of mankind. In the realms of God, in the World of Spirit there is no such thing as greatness, there is progression and that is all. There is ever the Way of Attainment and all who seek to tread that Way must first come into the full consciousness of what for you I must call Reality.

I wonder if you remember those beautiful words in the Scriptures, "Whatever thy hand findeth to do, do it with all thy might", and I think I might safely say that if there is any rule in Spiritual Life, that is the rule. There is no such thing as only seeking just what you desire. Desirelessness is one of the attributes of Spirit, but coming into this Way or Cycle of Necessity in this Earth Life, you have travelled along the Path of Evolution. You have gathered around yourself these qualities which are necessary so that you may use them in your earthly life.

God has always known that we would come to the point when we would seek to enter the density of Matter which we call the Earthly Life.

God knows that we, who indeed are already Spirit, clothed with the garment of the Soul, would eventually pass into that state of life where we would be surrounded by physical matter (flesh) and where we would use the body as a vehicle of expression. God therefore knowing that life upon the physical plane would be essential for us, has given us all that is necessary to take us along that Way. No man enters a plane of any sphere that is not prepared and you cannot come to an earth life, nor into any state or sphere until you are prepared for it.

Is it not a foolish thought to hold in our minds the concrete thought of not being able to accomplish or do that which we truly desire or find around us to do?

What the Spirit desires, we can always attain, for we could not be here today if we had not come to the point where all the qualifications necessary are already within us. We know that the Soul chooses its own way, that it sees the conditions that it desires to enter, before it does so, and it also sees and knows the qualities it has in order to live that particular life. We know that as the Soul travels the Path towards the world, that it is clothed with the garment that it will wear in the earthly life. It will bring into being all that it is, all the experiences it has been through in various spheres and state of life before, incarnations in various places and in various states, some of which we have memory beyond any doubt. Others can remember nothing and say that they "feel no answering vibrations in any state at all", and there is much questioning in the mind of man today about this and it can be explained thus and this is important. Only when it can be of value or of help does the knowledge of any state of life or existence come to you. It is not, as many people think and say, a matter of Evolution, nor is it a matter of being able to contact that state or vibration. These planes of matter can vibrate within us the consciousness of those conditions and we are able to bring that memory of them back with us into the earthly life and condition and "remember" them in our waking moments. Again, it is for more than that—the soul is impregnated with all the conditions, of all the states of life into which we have ever been, but again, there are many conditions in those states that it now becomes necessary to work through with complete unconsciousness of that previous state or time. For instance, one who at some time previously had held a position of authority may find any knowledge of that position completely withheld, because it may be that in this present day of life the entire memory of that power will be blotted from the consciousness of the physical mind, because of the vibratory force which it would set up in the earth today. It is not a personal matter, for we have to realise that this physical personality is a great barrier in the progress of evolution. So often memory is withheld, not because of the effect in *our* life, but because of the effect it would create in the ethers around others and in the world today.

Let us speak for a moment now of the Personal Self. Do you remember those beautiful words "whatever thy hand finds to do, do it with all they might", that is to say, with all the strength and all the Consciousness that is of God, for your might is your God Strength, your might is truly your Divine Consciousness, and if in your work, whatever it be, you are using that Divine Consciousness, you will not cavil or fret about the conditions in which you find yourselves. You will realize that as you truly are a part of that Great Force, wherever you are, whatever you are doing, if you use the God might that is within you, the Strength of God, you must of necessity bring all that work into a higher vibration of itself. You must in your workmanship realise the beauty within your true selves and that work can become a beautiful thing. It must, because a "thing of Beauty"—True Workmanship is the putting of yourselves into whatever you are doing. Remember again what I have said that you cannot be in any state of life at any time unless you are fitted to be there.

Only because the Personal Self rises up and seeks its own fulfilment does the Way of Life appear hard to you. Life is not hard. Life is beautiful. Because you bring to it the wrong conditions and because you approach it in the wrong spirit, does it appear to be hard. Perhaps as a child, as growing youth, as man or woman, you have held ideals of work, you have thought out your own careers and suddenly find it so different from what you imagined. Your lives seem forced into certain channels and you must work in the way you have been set to do. Your whole self, the physical being is perhaps crying out against the things you have to do, the conditions around you and those around you and the ways and means by which you must earn your physical living that provides you with your bread, food, clothing and well being, the creature comforts that you feel are so necessary to you.

You pray "give us this day our daily bread". Does it mean that you are only asking for what you think is necessary to live on? Perhaps, did you truly mean that when you asked for daily bread, God would give you strength to live in these conditions and using that strength make of life a "thing of beauty".

To raise the vibrations of the living force in life that all who live will feel there is true workmanship. To realise that wherever your physical desire or ideals may be, and if they be true, that you can bring them into whatever conditions you are placed.

The whole Spirit of your Being is Creative Force, and there can be no way of life in which you do not use that Creative Force. You live, move and have your Being—and these words are fraught with meaning, and if in shops and offices, homes and factories, if, in every way of Life you remember you live, move, and have your Being, you will perfect your work.

You remember the Master Jesus, and His Work. In the Spheres of Light He still works in the same way. He is never content to know that the thing is just well done, He seeks Perfection. He does not limit Himself to any sphere. He is in all and with all. None are too lowly for Him to seek, and none are too great to be at His side. There cannot be that setting of the one above the other, where there is a true desire for real workmanship.

Do you ever think or realise that workmanship is self abnegation? Do you ever think of what your work is going to mean in the thoughts of others, if you limit all you do to the merely physical round of this earthly life? This vibratory force that works can only remain in this condition, but surely if you realise that your hands, your feet, your lips and eyes, the whole of your physical senses are merely tools by which you can create, you *must* place within that work, whatever it may be, a glory, a beauty that will vibrate through all your life.

To be at one with your work is to produce true workmanship. I know you say, "I want to do so much and I feel that I could give so much, if only I were in the place that I want to be." Here it is that the personal self steps in, for the True Self, the Real Self, cannot be held or bound within any condition in which you find yourselves, and the True Self is seeking to express itself by creative force in whatever you do. To give of the True Self is to create and creating is not just a matter of using physical senses. It is a matter of using that Force, which is God. It is a matter of bringing into activity a Spiritual part, that is the real "I"! *Not* the little 'i' but the big 'I', the 'I' that has descended into matter, and reaching up, seeks to come again into the Spheres of Spirit. It is that 'I' you need to understand more about and it is the Personal Self that chafes against this, the Spiritual Self never does, for it knows that it has come into this World because it was its wish and right to do so.

So often you set out to be your own judges and say, "I could do better if I were in such and such a condition!" How do you know? Did He not say "Until ye become perfect in the little things, how can ye be perfect in the great things?" If you cannot or will not allow the Spiritual Force to flow through you, because the physical conditions are not to your liking, do you really believe that those same Spiritual Forces are going to flow more freely when you have all that the physical self is crying out for? If you do, then you deceive yourselves. They will not do so for if you cannot bring the Force of your Spiritual Self to function in all conditions, you limit it to the expression of the personal self, and then you bar the way for the Spiritual Self to come into the Way of Attainment, which can only mean one thing and that is not progressing, you are retrogressing. You cannot stand still, and wait and this is where the Spiritual Life differs from the Physical. When you say, "Oh, I'll just wait" do you realise what you mean? If you are not active and not using the Forces of Light and good that flow through you, then you begin to go back, you retrogress. It is from the Spheres of Activity that the forces in your own souls have come and if not used every moment of your lives, cannot stand and wait. They must return to their own spheres, for all things of good and progress dwell in these Spheres of Activity. They do not know inactivity and when you, by using free-will, deny the true self its right of expression then it must return to its own sphere to continue its work there. Later you will also return to that same condition and will have to work your way through it again.

You speak of *Death*—dead—means to you that which is *Inactive* and that is what so many people are—simply because they do not feel that life is right for them, or they do not possess those things of the physical that they think they should have, or are not free to do what they wish to do! God knows, God understands. He is ALL WISDOM and such is in His own keeping. He knows your way in life, He knows all your qualifications. You may *think* you do so, but remember, it is not given to you to know all that lies within your Soul. If you did there are times when you could not bear the might of that burden, and God, in

His Infinite Wisdom has given you the understanding that functions only on the planes where physical consciousness can be used. It is within you, and when you are separated from the physical body in the sleep state, that consciousness functions. You are aware of this, and you return into the physical body and earth life with the renewal strength of that wisdom.

Do not allow yourself to fall into the error of saying—"If I only knew more about myself?" You *do* know, all that there is to know if you would but let it rise. How are you going to do this? By good workmanship, by sincerity, by truth, by obedience, and by Love. Sincerity in what? In carrying out what truly lies within the Self and not always carrying out and fulfilling what you personally desire. If you sincerely desire to create in this the earthly world, that which is within you to create, then sincerely will you do it with your might, whatever your hand finds to do.

There is beauty in the simplest task, there is beauty that you may have shut away and hidden from the eyes of man. In all that you do, God's eye is over all. What do I mean by that? I will explain. You possibly believe that you can cheat yourselves in numerous ways, and still believe that you do not deny God in doing so. You say you do not mean to do so, but that is because you do not understand yourselves enough, but there is only Truth, or Untruth—no half way!

God has given each one Individuality, why then not express it? Spiritually you should know that you must use the self, and those forces which are yourselves, and by using them, go on to Higher things, using them in turn to grow, extend and express in order to attain. Individuality is fast becoming a lost attribute in the world. Imitating one another, doing something because another does it, or because you think by not doing it you will 'lose face' as it were, and yet many times you dislike anyone knowing you are doing these things. How weak you are, when you allow yourselves to be held by chains. Why limit the expression of your own individuality to the expression of another? Why not be yourself as you really are? Why set your lives by rules and formulae that other people express and lose your own Individuality? There was one who lived here, who said, "To thine own self be true, for it must follow, as night the day, if thou be not true unto thyself, thou canst not be true to any man."

William Shakespeare, a great and glorious light in the world, and if you study these words you will find many beautiful truths.

"To thine own self be true." That is what I am trying to teach you. You cannot be true to others if you are not true to yourself—if you follow the ways of those around you, if you deny God. You may feel it a strange thing to say, but it is true. God has given each his own self, his own Individuality, which is the expression of his own spirit. God set your feet upon the Path of Life. He said, "Go Forth and BE." He gave this path to tread that you might *BE*. If you are going to follow that which is entirely laid down for you by others, how can another say what is for you? They too can only follow the rules of Life. Only those, who by the Way of Evolution, have come into Spiritual Perception can possibly have any knowledge as to the best way of expression or the Self that is within. The Soul, having chosen its way, and seeking the earth life in which to express itself is sincere and desires to travel and to progress, taking the experiences it has gathered on its way to bring to fulfilment its own Spiritual desires.

That is life. Go into the depths of yourselves (your Souls), find out what you want to be and you will find the same desire to grow, for growth is of the Spirit. The Spiritual Self knows that you have, of necessity, come into conditions of life, where you will be able to express it, and you have the opportunity to do so. Therefore, no one has the right to say "I cannot give the best of myself, because of these conditions I am in,"—it is wrong. It is denying the God within and God is not limited by time, space, or by condition. God is the complete, perfect Force of Love.

Love is an expression and no matter where you are, or what you are doing no one can take away from you this power of expression. Remember always that if you put the best of yourselves into the work which you do, you create the opportunity to give more of yourself in a still better way. If your ideal is to be perfect, in so far as it lies in your power, you will not object to the means, or the methods that are used, to bring you to that Perfection. You will recognise in whatever conditions you are placed, there is the opportunity and remember also that *lost opportunities do not come again* in the same way. You grieve over failures, but you do not realise that if you fail you will have the opportunity to go on again, because if you have tried you have used the opportunity. You may not have fulfilled it, or you may have used only part of it, but it is not a lost opportunity but an opportunity that at least you have tried to use. Only because you fail to realise your own strength and therefore have failed to use it.

Lost opportunities only come again when you are set free from certain conditions of life, and you use your own creative force, your own true Self. If instead you limit your true force to the personal self, you will have lost your opportunity and it cannot come to you in that cycle of life again. It thus means that you could wait for a very long time to retrieve such an opportunity and that you will have to retrace your steps to even find it.

Many people here ask the question, "What will happen to us who have lost so many opportunities?" I would say to you—remember the Law of Compensation and remember that God understands. The All Loving Father knows your capabilities, knows your desires, and whether you use these or not. You may try to persuade yourself that you did not know or recognise the opportunity, but God knows how much knowledge there is within you and how much you are using it. Those who have been taught know of these powers that be within, know of these creative forces and can never deny this.

If you are sincere in your work, you will realise that you cannot be limited or bound by what you call your personal self in any work you undertake. Wishes and desires are dear to you and it is right that this should be so, since they are the echo of what is in the Soul. Do not be satisfied with the echo, but listen for the sound—the true sound of the Spiritual voice. The echo speaks so much of Self and self desire. So many beautiful things, so many beautiful words you speak, so many thoughts you have, but all of them overshadowed by the personal self. Seek in all ways of expression the True or Spiritual Self. It has no knowledge of littleness or greatness, but only recognises the "ALL" and that wherever you are, or whatever you are doing, is part of the "ALL". If you express that True Self that Creative Self, no matter what your task is, you will make of it a rare and beautiful thing and, moreover, you will be true to yourself.

Obedience is another quality that is essential to good workmanship. To obey, and by that I do not mean physical obedience, but the Spiritual aspect of a physical vibration.

Obedience is a necessity and a beautiful gift to have, and duty and obedience are not considered in the physical as being very different qualities. To be free is the term used in earthly expression rather than to be obedient, but obedience is a much greater thing and a much more beautiful jewel than freedom.

There is in the Spiritual Spheres, a great Hall that is called the "Hall of Jewels". It is here that words, phrases and various states of earthly life are shown as jewels in the "setting" of the Earth. They show their radiance and their dimness according to their vibratory force. The "jewel" counterparts in Spirit of Obedience and Freedom are really the same "jewel" but Freedom being the jewel that is of physical vibration and embedded in the Earth because it portrays physical desire, is dull, green in colour, and not bright but rather opaque, and takes the shade of the earth itself. Green, as you know, is the Highest Spiritual vibration that the earth is capable of producing, but its freedom does not shine with the radiance of the Spiritual Vibration, since freedom in its physical sense means the desire of the physical body and the unevolved part of the Soul. Freedom, in its Spiritual meaning is True Obedience, for Freedom, in its true Esoteric and Spiritual sense, can never come to you until you have learned obedience. The jewel of Obedience is very radiant, and reminds me of the earth gem, the topaz—a golden liquid, clear and shining bright, that gives forth strength and purity.

You must be obedient to the Higher Power of the God Force within yourself. You must train yourself to hear and know the Voice of the Spirit that is speaking within you at all times—to be obedient to it and only then can you attain Freedom. You can only obtain Perfect Freedom which is always the blending of that force and will that is Wisdom and Love, and there cannot be freedom until there is understanding. You cannot know the liberation of the soul until you know your Spirit, and until you know beyond any doubt what it is you are seeking, and that it is not the seeking of the things of the earth for only the personal self is satisfied with that.

Free—what do you mean by free? Do you not mean that part of you that wants to express itself, that wants to be at one with

God, and wants to see Him? It does not want to be suppressed —it wishes to express itself and cannot do so until the personal self has learned obedience. If you are not perfect in the little things, how can you be perfect in the great things? By the living of your lives, in the perfecting of your workmanship, you are expressing the God within you. By the limiting of your lives, no matter in what condition you are, you will never know Spiritual Freedom. Attain *Freedom* through *Obedience* to your Higher Self. Give your own being in whatever your hands find to do, and then you will, like the Beloved Master Jesus, never be satisfied with the thing that is just good or well done, you will seek to obtain perfection and in obtaining perfection come into the True Way of Light and be at—one with Him, who is All Light, All Love.

He will say, "It is well done, be of good cheer" and the gates of Light will open, the Radiance of the Spiritual Jewel of Freedom will come forth to meet you, and you will know in yourself the "Peace of God, that truly passes all understanding."

Chapter 8

THE GOING FORTH

This word was sounded many times by the Christ, in the Earth, when He sounded forth the "GOING" of His own Life. He also taught the full meaning of it to those who walked with Him—that word which is often on your own lips, such a small word, the word "GO"! Do you remember how many times He said *"Go* ye Forth", *"Go* your Way", "Go Hence", "Go"—. Words so often on His lips and used in His Life and I would like to try to bring a better understanding to you of the "GOING" in all Life.

All your lives are a "GOING". Let us just take the Spiritual Aspect of this Word. The GOING of the Spirit. When God wills that there should go forth from His Being the Spirit of His Life, He sends out into the Ethers, into the Planes that He chooses, the Very Breath of His Own Being. He sends forth upon the Way of Life, that Spirit of Love which is the Essence of God Himself, and in the Breathing forth, if He were to speak He would say, "Go out upon the Way of Life", Go out, and in the sounding forth of that Go(ing) He sends forth the Essence of Life, the Being of God, to manifest in the Planes of Life according to His Desire of Form. It is He who creates you all, it is He who sends you forth upon the Way, but He sends you forth in Love. Never forget that. You are sent out upon the Way, in Love, His Desire being that you should build and create, construct, and bring into manifestation in the forms of life in whatever plane it be—His Will. As He sent forth His Son into the Plane of Physical Life, to manifest forth His Being so He has sent you forth into these forms of life which He alone can make, only He can create.

You may shape—according to your powers to do so, and according to the plane of life in which you live, for He has given you that power. He has sent forth into you the Vibration of Life.

Whatever you are going to use to bring into form He has all the Consciousness of that thing. *You* may shape, but it is the *Will of God* within that creates that shape. You may live, but it is the *Breath of God* within you that gives you the right to live.

The Spirit came forth out of the Great All and that is what we call the Beginning of Life, Life in God, that is all our Beginnings. God breathed and said "GO FORTH", and the Spirit breathed forth was encased by the vibration of whatever vibration He chose to send forth. His Breath was the first vibration you could know, and as He breathed, His Will created about that Breath, a Force that would give the power to live in the planes He had created. At this point the Spirit sets forth upon its journey to the Planes of Life, clothed in the Vibration of His Breathing Forth, to the world which He also created. Do you ever think of your bodies as the first garment of the Spirit which God created for you and in which you live today? God made these and He knew then the Way that you would travel. He knew the Power of the Vibratory Force He was sending forth, and He knew that in that Vibration there was the power that would carry it through all the Planes of Consciousness and eventually return it to Him and there is the Promise of Life! This bringing together of all the great promise of Beauty, Hope and Goodness that you can ever think of. "Ye shall return". He has said that you have His Power, His Love, His Force, that will bring you back to Him. Can you lose hope for others with the thought of that? Can you not look upon the most hardened sinner—I say sinner because that brings to you what I want to convey—he who has for a time lost his vision of God, who cannot see clearly the Light, and only watery sunlight and not the true Rays of God in his life—and see that in their lives. Can you remember that whatever they do, wherever they go, whatever they are, God has said "Go forth and ye shall return to me." There has never yet been a creation of God, that He has not put into it His Force that will return and be at-one with Him. There is the "True Promise of Life." "Go Forth that ye may return to me" and the Spirit is encased in the promise.

It enters the plane of Soul Life clad in the garment of that promise that will bring you back, no matter where you travel, whatever you may become, whatever you may do, whatever your sufferings, always there is this gleam of hope that will never fade or die. There is the one Eternal Promise that will live throughout your lives that you will return to Him and setting forth there on your journey, clad in the garment of God, you enter the Plane of Experience.

You came into the *Soul Planes* first and you begin to use those *senses* that God has given you. These *Senses* are not like the senses you are using now, but the senses that are aware of *all* things in *all* vibrations. God has found it necessary for the perfecting of the manifestation of His Force on the Planes of Life with those whom we call the human race. The souls, that are men and women, who will help Him in the evolving of the forces over which He gave them the right to rule. They will touch every Plane of Life, and will pass through using their Divine Will and their Divine guidance, which is vibrating with them through that garment that He wove. They shall then know the power of all the senses manifesting in the Soul Plane.

Then in the *Mental Plane* and finally into the *Planes of Physical Life* where you must use all your senses for all Soul sensing both here and in the Soul Planes is not limited to the kingdoms to which they belong. They are extremely sensitive and react to the manifestations of all forms of matter and life in *other* forms. They find in the Soul Planes that there are many vibrations of many forms (you will already know that everything and everyone has their own particular vibration) and are aware of them, they also realise that they can be one with them and understand them. They can see, know and feel in the Higher form all those senses, all the conditions into which they enter and through which they pass. They become, in other words, aware of the senses of the Soul Force. They find they have a body, with the vibrance of that first garment in which God clothed them and from that they are aware of the power to use, to create and to serve and that there are those around who will help them to understand all the things with which they come into touch. They will find Helpers and Guides. They will find seekers who have been in the darker planes of life, and who, realising this condition and the cause, are now on the Path back to God. They will meet those who have passed through the Planes of Experience (Earth life), which they themselves have yet to touch, and they will become aware of the Force within them also. They will be able to vibrate to those fellow travellers and they will learn from them what they have done, what they have found, and what use they were able to make of the senses they received.

This is exactly as you, here in the Earth Plane, meet others who have travelled to other and perhaps strange lands. They tell of life, conditions and customs, of life quite different from us, how they use their talents in different ways. They can also tell you whether they were able to use their gifts in their own way, and of all the other experiences which they encountered. So, in the Soul Plane there is even that "Going" and "Coming". The Souls who are beginning their life's journey are "Going Forth", and those who have passed through the states of life's experiences are going back. "Going" is the true vibration of life, for life is in truth a journey and full of experiences which help the Soul to become more Vibrant with the Force that God has given—using God given strength. This strength or force passes into many planes of Soul Consciousness, to many Halls of Learning and States of Being—it passes into spheres and planes and ever and always there are those more advanced who will help them to understand. There is never any condition or state of being in the Soul life, that there are not those who are able to explain, able to help and able to strengthen and point the way for you.

In the states of Soul Consciousness, there are always the opportunities to use all the forces of which you become aware to enable you to reach a higher state of perfection, or to sink to a lower state of being. That which we call "Freewill" begins to operate from the moment the garment of God clothes the Spirit. In all states of consciousness there is no holding back, there is knowledge, for you have started out with wisdom, and the first duty, if I may call it so, of the Spirit, is to see that the Force of Wisdom passes into the body, or the garment of the Soul, and given Inner Force or Power to take into itself the consciousness of its own Spiritual Being and its own capabilities.

How much aware are you of your own possibilities and your own potentialities? The Spirit has Wisdom and Wisdom seeks to send into the Soul enough of itself to allow the Soul to touch and to know all the conditions through which it passes and to give it complete consciousness of how those experiences may be used. It is the Work of the Spirit in all Planes of the Soul, that as you come into the Consciousness of your own Being you are perfectly aware of the Forces of God within, how you can use them and touch all states and conditions and choose for yourselves whether you will follow the Light, or turn aside from it. You set out on the broad pathway of Life, but from that Pathway there are many deviations smaller and what appear to be attractive bye paths that you could travel, but if you are using the Wisdom of the Spirit, you will also know that you must keep straight on the *broad* pathway and not deviate from it. If you do, you will find that you only have to retrace your steps to find the right and true pathway that your own Soul demands of you. It was never meant that man should always walk on the sunlit Path of Life—for that is not the Way of God or the way of All Progress.

Growth can only be produced by the drawing together of all forces, for He gave the power to transmute all things that were not progressing in the Way of Progression and so bring darkness into light.

Wander down these side paths that deviate from the Truth, find and taste many things and many desires, but always the Force of God, the first garment of the Soul, vibrating within you the Power of God, the power to choose and seek that which is of Light Right, and good, that which is essentially Truth and Beauty will bring you back eventually to the right Way. Then you will know without any doubt that the power of the Spirit, the Essence of God permeates all things even in your experiences of the "not good" way of life. All the Soul Life is a Way of Preparation—all the ways of life must be. For some there are deeper experiences, to many they are not so intense, but you are never allowed to suffer or enjoy any experience without being fitted to endure it all. The Father does not send His children out unprepared, and if you always remember this you cannot fail and your courage cannot fade, and above all you cannot lose hope.

Now Faith—you know that word only too well and it is difficult to feel that people on the whole possess this quality. Do you think and live Faith? If you listen to the words many people use and the amount of empty soundings made, it would appear that there is very little faith, for the Soul has no use for words and words alone! It wants and needs action, for true action is creation.

The physical plane of living that we know as the Earth World is dense in matter and glorious in its beauty. God created it all and mankind. When man came into the world in his physical body he also was given the Force of God to use, the power of dominion over the kingdoms and the ruling of those kingdoms. When you pass through the states of soul consciousness, and learn to use them for "good" or "not good" you come at last into the kingdom and "rule". Do you realise this? What has He in reality said—? Is it not "Go forth and take the power of mind and body and in my Kingdom of the World manifest through this garment of flesh that I have given you. Use my Power to create, speak the Word, vibrate forth my Being and out of those vibrations will rise and live forms of life upon the earth. Go forth and make it yours, go out into my World I give it to you. I have created it for you. I am your Father and you are my Child and in that world you can live, build and create new worlds that will live for all Eternity. Do you see the parallel in the physical world of Mother, Father, Child?" Do you see them saying, "Go out into the World and live your life." I, we, your Father, Mother, the one the male, female element, which alone can create perfect form, we have created you by God's Will, He gives us that power. Now! go forth and live!

Can you not see the glory and beauty of it? The repetition of God's miracle of Being, the human elements of Life. The Father-Mother saying to the child, "We will show you the Way", "We will teach you how to use your body and your mind", for we have lived in this life and travelled the pathway of life, and can show you what all these senses and forms you have are for. The Father and the Mother have the right to train the child and show it how to use its limbs. The Father and Mother sets the child upon its feet, teaches it how to walk, teaches it balance of life, to carry its body in harmony with others around it so that it may "Go Forth" and do its work upon the earth. The way of physical life is another "Going Forth" on a journey—but still the same Going Forth to gain the knowledge and consciousness of how to use the physical things, to learn the real things of living and shedding those that are but the shadows and unreal.

You drop the baby garments as the baby grows to childhood and when you grow to manhood the same process, and so it goes on.

The garments are fashioned so that they are suited to the days work or to the occasion you know, if they are not so you will feel uncomfortable and it will have an effect on your feelings and mental body so that you are unable to express yourself adequately. The weaving of garments best suited to yourselves is a very vital matter, because you have taken on yourselves in the vibratory force that which will best be attuned to the task you are going to perform. Always remember that what you are wearing is a part of yourself for your emanations pass through it. It is an outer form of matter, therefore it will be through this garment that the emanation of your actions will go in to the things you touch and handle.

And so you go forth into the physical way of life into the Cycle of Necessity as we call it, well equipped for the journey and to use the knowledge you have gained in the states of consciousness, to use also the vibrance of the garment, of Wisdom that God gave to you when He sent you forth, vibrating all the time into the physical body and mind. The mind and body take in new vibrations in that sending forth until you come to the end of physical life and you go forth again to die. Do not forget the vibration of the physical sound of "forth to die". Do not think of death, but truly of "Going Forth"—another part of the journey—the return journey to God. There in the physical day of life, every condition, every event, every hope, every disappointment, every achievement, every failure, is a part of the Way of God. You go on your Way and will go forth out of the physical body and enter again the Soul Planes, the mental and conscious states of being. You realise what you have done, what use you have made of all the "garments" God gave to you, of the things He gave you to help your travel on the Way, and according to that realisation you go on, or seek to return again, but whatever you do, you will "Go Forth", or you will go back, but always "Go".

You will perhaps "Go" after many many incarnations, in many forms and in many planes of life, but one day you will go into the Great Plane of the Christos and know yourself to be truly a Child of God. "Go Forth, that ye may return"—Always "Going". Remember the example of His Love. God said to Him "Go Forth". He went and He returned and so shall we.

Chapter 9

SOUND

When the first Christians came together, awaiting what their beloved Master and Leader had taught would come to them, they were in the Upper Room. He had said that, before they went out into the physical planes of life and living, to begin their ministry of teaching and to continue what He had begun, they would receive the gift of the Holy Spirit. Force would enter them and all that He had taught them of the inner meaning of life and its ways, of all the wisdom, which He had given to them concerning the Spiritual Way of Life, would be touched by the Force. The centres of their inner bodies would receive that Force of Light, which would quicken them into that higher rate of vibration, so that from the moment of reception, they would ever be at one with their Master, in the Spheres of Life, Love and Wisdom. They would go forth to teach His people, having received that quickening Force of the Spirit.

They waited in the silence, in which He had taught them always to wait, to receive that great blessing, which they did not seek for themselves, but for which they waited with great joy. Well did they know that it was to be the beginning of the great work, which He had left for them to do. He had taught them that He would never leave them, even though the physical form, in which He had had His Being for so long, were to pass from life. That part which was truly Himself, and which they had never lost for one moment during their travels with Him would still be present in their midst; but they would not become aware of it, in its true force, until their inner centres had been fully opened.

So long as He walked with them, there was not the same need for that Force to be used; but when He went thence, it would be necessary for them to use that Force, so that they too could, in their giving forth of the teachings, use the vibrations, we know as sound, to penetrate, not the *minds* of those who listened to them, but the depths of their souls, and touch the Spiritual Being that lives in all mankind. So, each one of you must come to the truth, when the Holy Spirit will function in and through you. In the silence you learn to know sound!

Sound is vibration, as colour and number are also vibration. When you place sound, colour and number together you have form, for there is no form in your life, throughout this plane of earth which does not contain sound, colour and number.

You are taught to believe that all sound comes forth in physical form, but the most far-reaching sounds, that are produced in the earth, are not the sounds made by lips. The sounds produced by your spiritual self, in your looks, your actions, the tones of your voice, can travel through all the spheres in this plane in which you live and through many spheres beyond it, according to their power to do so.

If you vibrate in the physical planes of life, holding yourself bound by the physical, you will sound forth only the notes of the physical life which can vibrate in these planes only. Your own Spiritual Being cannot hear these sounds. They are too dense and cannot reach the higher planes. When man lifts himself and seeks to know the infinite life, deny it, as he may, with his lips and his life, he will know within himself, the ruling Force of all Life. Then will he give forth sounds that will travel through all spheres, for they will be the vibration of the great Spirit of Life, Himself. In music you play one note, and the eighth note above that you call the octave. This is the same sounding except that the octave is a finer and higher sounding in its vibratory force than the lower one. So it is with your lives. The first sound is your physical life, and over this is the greater Soul/Spirit force, that will vibrate in your lives if you allow it.

You were sounded forth into the vibratory force that you call life. You came into being as sound, as vibration. All through your life, in your spheres of soul-consciousness, in your passing through the many planes of consciousness and in your entry into the physical plane of existence, you vibrate constantly in your higher self to that note which was your sounding forth. As you travel on your way, you gather around you the vibratory forces of many conditions and it is for you, the descending and ascending soul, to choose which note of your octave, you will sound forth.

In the choice of colour, you may often choose one that pleases only your senses. You may feel, perhaps, that you are happier in that specific colour or that your appearance is improved by it, but that is only the vibration of the physical self, or of that part of the soul that has come into being in this plane to seek its way; but it may not necessarily be that the colour which you like, is the colour that is going to be of the greatest help to you in the evolving and progression of your soul!

You have to learn to know yourself! You must learn to be able to feel, not the satisfaction of the physical mind and body, but the deeper sense of peace that comes within you when the true vibration or colour ray is being used by you.

As you use your colour, you also use your sound. As you become attuned to the true vibratory force of colour, you also become attuned to sound, for every colour *must* sound its note and as it sounds its own note in the harmony of that chord in which you are "Being", then you will be able to take from it *all* the Force which will help each part of you to vibrate along that scale, until you ascend to that highest note of the octave, making a complete chord in the harmony of your life. You will then be able to pass to the next higher note in the evolution of your higher self.

All through the Old and New Testaments of the Bible, if you read, seeking to understand not just the words that are given but to catch the notes that are being sounded, you will learn to appreciate more fully the rhythm, harmony and vibration of all that is taught there. You will find in many stories, the symbols of how in the beginning and throughout the Bible the consciousness of man burst forth into song or wept and wailed, struggling as now to understand himself and to place himself in harmony with the true laws of Life.

In the earth plane of life today, there is noise, more and more noise and the vibration of noise. The world calls that noise sound!

Go out into the fields and the woods! Go away from Towns and Cities! Go, if you can, into the silence of nature! There you will find sounds that will vibrate *within* you—not the sounds of towns, shops, factories, offices or houses, nor the sounds of people concerned about their own recompense—but the sounds of the True Force of Life, giving and pouring forth its love, truth and wisdom, strength and beauty. Listen to the notes which the birds sound for you! They do not sing because they desire praise from those who may hear them. There may be dozens or hundreds of them singing together, but you do not hear any finding fault. You do not see any looking around to discover which is producing more or better sound than they. They sing and pour forth their being in Love.

Could you but hear with the physical ear, as you hear with your inner senses, the sound of growing grass, of trees, leaves, of flowers or the sounds of running water, you would find in them the true vibration of sound. You would find the giving not the seeking. They produce, not because they desire praise or gain but because it is the expression of the very essence of their life. That is what all sound should be.

You are taught that in the beginning the Great Spirit spoke the Word. By the sounding of the Word, all things, which today you know in life were produced. By sound the human race was first brought into being and it is by sound that today everything around you is being created. The ethers are filled with vibration which you call sound. Only when man reaches a better understanding of the power that lies within him to create sound, will he cease to be satisfied with the harsh notes that are being vibrated in the living of his life, or in the producing of his words, but he will seek to give forth a gentler sound but not necessarily a weaker one, for in noise is weakness but in gentleness is strength!

Why has man produced today's clamour? It is but the outward striving to attune the sound of his own inward inspiration to his spiritual aspiration. He has not yet succeeded in understanding his seeking because to him the desire for something is a pure physical getting or gaining. He is turning these sounds into a physical vibration. The world is becoming bound by discordant notes that you are taught to recognise as sound. Great efforts have been made by Masters and Messengers from the world of Spirit, to form in this plane of life, centres from where a better understanding of sound should come. They seek to bring to the physical minds of men, a greater feeling of harmony. For that purpose they are using rays which are touching the hearing centres. They are trying by these forces to attune the physical organs to a better vibration of sound. It is the desire of those who seek to help that you should become dissatisfied with the sounds that are being produced around you, and that through that dissatisfaction there will come the desire to create a pleasanter sound in harmony with the higher vibration of your own hearing organs, and thus gradually, there will come to this earth plane the sounding of the true vibration, that holds true colour, true sound and true number and which will then produce perfect form.

The earth world and all that lives there today is restless. There is no calm. Some of you say, "Yes, I have found calm. *I* know how to be calm and peaceful." Are you sure? Generally what you call calm is but an outer semblance. While your body and your mind may be at rest, there is still a turbulent soul tumbling and pouring over its obstacles. In all the vibrations of life today, where do you find calm? When you know the true peace of your own spiritual being, your ears will be attuned to that calm and peace. You will seek to attune all things of life to the true vibration of sound and in vibrating forth *that* sound you will give to others the opportunity to do so also.

The Father-Mother of all Life spoke the Word that created what you know today as Life. It was, and still is, the desire of the Father-Mother, the Great Spirit, God, the Giver of Life, that you too will create the harmony of beauty, peace and love by the vibration of sound. To sound your note is to know your Spiritual being.

There are those who teach their pupils what they call mantrams. They take words and phrases and place them together. Out of the rhythm of the physical meaning of these mantrams, which the student is taught to pronounce or repeat, they teach that life will become more simple, that greater understanding will come as a result of the repetition of these sounds placed together in physical form. If it is only the physical mind that is sounding forth those words, how can they bring the peace and calm of the Spirit? If they are vibrated forth, they will but sound forth into matter, which is of itself and will indeed bring back peace and calm, but only on the same vibration as themselves. If you were never to make a sound of speech, but were to vibrate through the sounding forth of your Spiritual self, you would then bring back to yourself the peace and the calm of the Spirit.

Is not too much importance being placed on the earth sounds and not enough on the sound of the Spirit? The Spirit sounds forth in silence! Many times you say, "I have tried to help this or that person but I cannot. They will not listen to me. I have talked to them, but still they will not listen." Is it not in the very words that the one you try to impress and to help has been turned aside? If you are forever knocking on a door of wood, in time your hand with which you knock will become like that wood. It will become hardened. So it is with physical sounds! With the physical desire to impress you make the sound as of wood, and you will not have the power to vibrate more than these same physical sounds. Try to realise that the sounding forth of the true spiritual sound is to understand that not only physical words carry forth sounds, but the look that is within your eyes, the movements of your body are all vibrating sounds.

If I were to raise my arm, and you had the ear of Spirit, you would hear the sound of that movement. To your physical ear, it is a soundless one, but even as the hand of flesh and blood is raised or lowered through the ethers, it is producing the vibratory force of its own element. According to the vibration of life in physical form, so this vehicle, in physical form of flesh and blood, will emanate and vibrate into the ethers the sound which it alone can produce from the force which I use. Have I raised my hand in anger, then it will vibrate anger. Have I raised it in peace, blessing or understanding then their vibration will flow from it. Have I raised it in love, then it will vibrate love. Have I held it out and touched something to satisfy the forces of the body, then that vibration will be transmitted. Have I held out my hand to receive only to satisfy the self and the senses of physical life, then as the earth life things are touched, that vibration will be instilled into them. What a personal responsibility is ours!

Listen to the physical sounds when next you go into the streets! Listen to the footfalls and you will be able, by your understanding, to sum up the character of the person making these sounds. You will be able to say to yourself, "There goes one who has this or that characteristic in his physical life." Listen also to the vibration of the impact of these feet upon the streets and you will be able to say, "There goes one who leaves vibrations which will raise or lower the evolution of the next person who touches it."

Seek to open wide within you the gates of your own Spiritual wisdom that you have a better understanding! Sound is not just a physical giving forth of physical manifestations, through form. Sound is the vibratory force of your life! So long as you measure your life by sound, that is by speech, so long you will limit your life to the physical planes of being. Begin to understand that sound has colour and number! All three vibrations are of the one, vibrating as one, for the perfect triune is in these three forces. They are manifestations of God, of the All-Spirit in physical being. You will know with that understanding that every sound that you produce is limited or unlimited according to the way it is sounded forth. If it is a sounding from your physical life, it can only remain in that vibration. If it is the sounding forth of the soul that is seeking to progress, then it will vibrate to that soul-matter and there it will find its own octave. It will find the highest note of its own physical octave, and so pass into the next one, which is the higher form of evolution. If it be a Spiritual sounding forth that you make in your lives, then not only will it be the complete octave of your physical being and your soul expression but it will be the perfect harmony of your own note, colour and number. You will be manifesting forth the vibratory force in perfect harmony with all your own life, in spirit. If you would really seek to understand the true harmony of life, attune your ears to the inner sounds that are around you. Do not be content to listen with the physical ear to physical sounds that are being made, but ever seek by your own Spiritual force to hear the sounds that are constantly being produced around you, in what you call the silence. You say that you withdraw into the quiet. You speak of seeking the silence, yet if you understood yourself, if you had the wisdom of your own being, you would know that in the noisiest part of the earth world you could be in complete silence. You would not need to be withdrawn. You need to go apart for "going apart" means that you are still a part of all that is, and so you are conscious not only of your relationship in physical terms with all that is around you, but you are also aware in your spirit of being a part of all that is With that understanding comes the hearing ear. The same applies to the eye, the eye that does not only look upon form and see form, but the eye that sees in every form the inner part, as the ear is attuned to the inner vibration of all things.

How many times do you speak to people and expect them to understand what you say? You cannot speak what you do not mean! The words that you use are a part of you. No-one else can produce these. Truly, you may not mean, in your inner or spiritual self what you have said, but there is a part of your physical consciousness, or sub-consciousness that is part of your soul functioning, that has created within you what is sounding forth, for your sound is but the emanation of what has been within and which you have created. You have taken it out of the emanation in which it lives and brought it into being, within a physical force. Try to understand your own powers to create! You know that in the physical world a sound can break a vessel. It can shatter it to pieces. Remember that the sounds which you produce in your words can break lives, can create discord that will shatter to thousands of pieces, forces that are being built up in life! Do you realise that as you laugh and jest among yourselves, that many times these laughs are brought forth into the planes of life through spoken words that are unclean? Thoughts are being created into impure words, and you laugh?

Your physical senses create laughter, such laughter as only darkened souls can hear, but listen! Listen to the laughter that ripples forth from the Spiritual Being of an innocent babe! Listen to the little one who cannot yet distinguish one physical thing from another, but only knows what responds to its own inner being! Could you but listen now, with your inner ears, and hear the vibrant laughter of a child rippling forth, not caring who hears it, because from within itself joyousness comes forth. That is the sound of the Creator!

Listen to the bird as it sings and you hear again the sound of the Creator! It is joined by another and yet another and you will hear harmony produced by thousands of voices in little throats. You will hear song, that seeks to give utterance only to that which is itself—joy and love. Seek to understand *that* sound, and you will not be so eager to give forth the sounds of your physical voices! Why speak so many words? Why talk, talk with physical voices! Most of the time, the physical minds are not in harmony with your words and your spiritual thoughts cannot be heard.

Noise, created by your own physical desire in the physical brain of the self, is so loud, so gross in its vibration, that the finer vibrations of your own Spiritual being are lost within yourself, and you cannot produce them.

Study very well your own voice! Go into a room by yourself and, standing close to one of the walls, speak words! Speak words as you would speak them to another physical being, and listen not only with your physical ears but try to catch all the vibrations of what you are sounding! Listen well, not only with your ears, but with your perception, to the sounds you hear around you! You will hear false notes being struck. You will hear, all through the ethers of these planes, those sounds that are physical. Only now and again will you catch the true note, the true vibration. When you do, you will not hear it with your physical ears. You will hear it with your inner self. You will feel within yourself the flowing forth, for *your* Spirit will have sought the sound of Spirit, and will respond to it.

There must be a sounding forth in all lives, not by words of flesh but by the living, the being of the Spiritual Self. Those sounds will take all impurities and purify them. They will contact all those who are weak and faint with the burden of their own life and strengthen them upon their way.

Let us ask of the Great Spirit that into the wisdom of our own Being shall flow understanding of what we call sound that we may, each one, go forth and sing our Song of Life to all mankind upon these earth planes!

CHAPTER 10

SOUL PROGRESSION

We often hear the words, "It is the desire of my soul to do this or that." What is really meant when this is said?

The desire of the soul is for freedom, love and creation. The soul cannot become free until the power of the spiritual consciousness is used in the daily living of life! It wants freedom from all that holds it back on the path of purity and light. It has chosen to come into a dense body of matter (the flesh), because it knows that, in that dense body of matter, it will be given the opportunity to liberate itself for all eternity from the forces it has wrongly created.

When conditions seem wrong many Chelas say, "They may be in my Karmic force. Am I never to be freed from them in this life?"

Would it not be better to say, "I know not whether I shall be liberated in this day of life; but if I can liberate myself by my own Spiritual force in this earthly day of life, I can, and will, use the force of the Spirit that will prepare my soul for the liberation, when it has gained the strength to be so liberated."

If you know, if you feel, or even if you have been told, by Spiritual Forces that you are bound at this present time by Karmic force of the mind or the body, do you ask yourself each earthly day of life as you come to its ending what you have done to purify your thoughts, to attain the mastery of your mind, to liberate yourself physically and mentally from the mastery of others' minds? If there be Karmic force within your body, how much have you sought each day to use the power of the Spirit to liberate the atomic structure of your own physical body from the thraldom of that hold?

These are the forces that you must use if you seek the freedom of the soul. You must endeavour to listen to the counsel of your own Spiritual self. Know yourself, not as others think they know you, but know yourself by the wisdom of the Spirit, for that is true knowing. Know how much or how little you have used the true force of the soul. Each day as you set forth you say to the Great Spirit that you seek strength in the Path of Service, but how far does that carry you? Every time that you say, in the silence of your spiritual being, and in the silence of your soul, "This day I would serve my God!" then in the asking or the voicing or the sounding forth of these vibrations, you have attracted to your own self every mis-creation of your Karmic path. You have called into action every weakness of the atomic structure of your etheric body. You have called into active being every weakness of the flesh, every force of the not-good that seeks to overthrow the Kingdom that is truly the Heaven of God. You have not only called it into action in your own life, but in all Planes of Life. You may react to this and say, "What a dreadful thought!" Say rather, "What a great and glorious moment! What a glorious thought! God gives to us, His children of earth, the power of life, His power, to create anew!"

How good it is to know that in this hour of the great evolution, the great Master of All has let us come forth to hear again the soundings of the great Christ Force upon the earth, "Behold, I, the Great Spirit, make all things new!" It is by using the creative spirit and principle in your life, that you will find the great freedom of the soul.

Physical people so often are rather too fond of their faults and weaknesses. They are too glad, maybe, to be looked upon by others as being weak, weak in the using of strength physically, mentally or soulfully. There is no such thing as the sin of spiritual pride; but there is sin, the sin of the soul, the sin of those who say, "I know I have weaknesses that I cannot overcome. I want to overcome them but cannot!" That is the sin of loving your own faults! That is the sin that someday will grow to such a strength that you will not recognise it as such, so much will it have become a part of you! Find that strength that you have created upon the Karmic path of life! Search well and find the power of the Christ which brings you strength from the spheres beyond this earth! For you who have come upon this earth plane, who have stood at His altar and said, "I would go hence into the Planes of Matter. I would descend again into the density of these planes, where I may take upon myself the Karmic forces of all life, and by the purity of Thy light, cleanse and make new all that has become darkness." For you, rejoicings rang forth on all the planes of light in that moment. Remember that when next temptation comes to you in mind or in body! Remember that you have stood at the Altar of Light, and have cried, "I would go hence, O Master of All Light, to bring light in the darkness, to re-create with Thy light all that is of darkness. "There you will find strength to give freedom to your soul, freedom to liberate its very Karma that it has created, freedom to walk the Path of Light in purity of being, freedom from the power of the flesh and freedom from the power of the mind. Remember that this is the battle that will never cease until you stand within His light!

You will have to fight powers of the mind and body as long as you live upon the planes of earth, for you have come in service unto God and therefore unto man. So long as there is one thought of self, one thought of the desire of self, you will fight and fight to find the light, the purity and the strength to liberate your soul, which is the Soul of all.

When you experience each day the weakness of the flesh or mind, and your struggle leaves you trembling in the physical body, weakened in your physical strength, do you think that *your* fight is the fight of many millions of souls upon the earth today? Do you think of the power of re-creation, that you can send forth every day till you come to your knees before God and in the silence of your spiritual being cry, "Help me in my hour of weakness to purify and take upon myself the Cross of the Flesh!" Christ in his agony cried, "If it be Thy will, O Father, that I should pass this way, grant me of Thy strength, that for the sake of all mankind to come, I shall drink of the dregs of this cup." (These were His words to the Father, however distorted they became by the teachings of mankind). Are you greater than He, that you cannot cry to the Father in your agony and torment of mind and body? Let your cry for help ring out to Him who is all Wisdom and all Love.

If you truly seek the freedom of the soul, cast off that mantle and cloak of self. Blend the power of the Christ into your weakness and into your strength and He will give you what you seek. Freedom of the soul can never come from the strength of the mind or of the body. It can only come from the spirituality of your own life. Be not weary in the fight! There are millions who fight in the earth today, wearied, so wearied, yet ever eager and ever desirous of overcoming evil. What is it that makes them fight? What is it that holds *you,* in *your* hour of trial and hardship when your physical body is sometimes in danger? To what was it you turned, and whence came your strength? Was it from your mind and body? No! It was from the depth of your spirit, whenever the physical part of you was fearful.

Many have faced dangers from physical weapons of great power. In many parts, the dangers that beset you at that time have left their vibrations in your towns and cities. Your mind, too, is still attacked by the vibratory forces of threats to home, town and safety. You, who are a student of the inner teachings of Life, you who have sought the Way, have set your feet upon the Path and therefore your soul knows that you must help in the liberation of those souls who used such weapons to your home, town and city. Your soul knows that you must help, that you will free yourself in the freeing of those souls whose minds created these forces and forged these weapons that brought destruction to the earth planes of Life.

People met together and thanked the great Father that the danger which was with them for a time was over; but you, who understand truth, know that the forces that were liberated in those day and night hours were not only physical weapons. In them were the forces of souls in torment, who, in the Astral Planes today, are seeking to overthrow the Kingdom of Power and Light. Therefore, they are still brought to the planes of earth. They are a part of *your* way. The words you speak, the thoughts you think, are the forces that will liberate and give freedom to your soul and to the souls of all men on this plane and to the souls in darkness in these spheres.

Freedom for your soul is the first step to the mastery of self. Recognise the Karmic Force, not only of *your* life but of the lives of all the Karmic forces of the nations, the Karmic forces of the mineral, animal and vegetable kingdoms, the Karmic forces of all races of mankind. To recognise these forces is to recognise and realise that you are one of them. Every time that you, by the power of the living force of the Christos, raise one vibration of darkness out of the lower form into the higher, you have vibrated *your* voice to the sounding of His, "Behold! I make all things new! "

CHAPTER 11

THE LAW OF CAUSE AND EFFECT
or
SPIRITUAL PROGRESSION AND THE MASTERY OF SELF

To obtain a deeper realisation of the possibilities of spiritual progress in this earthly life, one must become more aware of the opportunities to do so, which arise day by day and which are, too often, unnoticed. By realising, in your ordinary life, the possibility of furthering the advancement of your spiritual welfare, you attune your vibrations to all that is good, and so good will come with every fresh opportunity day by day. Many are not aware of this. Very often they will not consider the things that happen to them worthy of thought, because they have been trained to consider anything which does not bring physical or mental ease and comfort or material gain as unworthy of their consideration, and it is dismissed from their minds. If you, however, have discovered a fuller understanding, not only of your own powers, but of your true desires, then you will ask for whatever is for the betterment of your soul's progress. You will not be daunted by what we term failure, which is so often not failure, but rather a lack of using the full strength within you.

How often have you fought to gain a certain point of view, or to put certain plans into action? How often have you examined and re-examined your thoughts and actions? How often have you felt that you ought to stand by certain rules for the conduct of your own life, only to give way under a sudden fit of depression or of strong desire, or for fear of other people's opinions, and you reverse your decisions and resume your old ways? How much happier have you been by doing so? I venture to say that you were not happier. Indeed, I'll go further and say that you became restless, dissatisfied, depressed and conscious, deep down in your heart, that you had betrayed your higher self to satisfy the human element.

Well, it is never too late to transmute wrong to right. If you begin by putting right what you know to have been wrong in your life, you will have made a good start on the path that leads to your goal, for you will be dealing with the Law of Cause and Effect, which must vibrate in all lives.

How much have you helped other people by doing what *you* thought they wanted you to do? Have you thought of the Karmic forces that you set in motion in their lives? I am sure you have not, for if you thought seriously of the effect which you have created in thought and deed, you would never have done it.

Half measures are very poor efforts! When you find that you are, metaphorically speaking, patting yourself on the back and feeling that you really have done a good deed, just pause for a moment and ask yourself if it really was a good deed. Seek a parallel in the life of the Master when He lived here, and you will quickly find your answer. You have been taught, "Thou shalt have no other God but me" and "You cannot serve two masters". You must be the master of your seeking, progressing self, or it will be *your* master. Which is it to be? Only *you* can answer that, and you can only answer truthfully when you turn the light of spiritual progress upon your question. Are you truly seeking the mastery of self, or is the opinion of people around you and the desires of your own self still uppermost in your life?

By now, you are probably saying to yourself, "How am I to know? I feel I am doing what is right. It is so difficult to see what is wrong! "

I do not agree with you. You say these things because you have not yet gone into the depths of your own knowing. Remember how often the Master went apart to seek a clearer seeing, a surer guidance than His earthly mind could give! Do you remember that he was scoffed and jeered at, criticised and condemned by those who knew Him? Did He allow that to alter His ways? Never! He always held fast to that which was good and His Father and His Father's laws were His guide. He taught that seeking should be within the true self, not weighed by earthly measure but by spiritual laws. The fault lies within us, for we still continue to use the earthly measure of things and people. We allow ourselves to be weighed down by earthly ways of thinking and living. We shall never attain the true mastery of self until we, too, go apart and measure all our deeds and thoughts in the light of God. We wish each other "Good Health", but that is not always good, if we mean what we say, for in physical language that means we are wishing them ease from bodily suffering. Yet, as esoteric students well know, thousands of souls have incarnated today to take into their earthly bodies disease and suffering, so that by bearing and enduring them in the strength of the Father, they may transmute that disease into harmony. You know, too, that many thousands are suffering in mind and body as the result of injuries done to some of the elements of which the mind and body are composed, in other states of being and they are working through a Karmic force to attain purity.

When you wish each other "Good Health", make your thought one of spiritual purity, that your hope for them is that they will in their living attract to their souls and bodies the constructive forces that will build up their Etheric bodies, and that will supply them with the strength required for the task that they have chosen.

It would be well if you gave much deeper thought to the true meaning of your utterances! It is not necessary to voice all your thoughts, but if they are constructive, aspiring, born of true spiritual seeking to give service, then *you* will know what you mean by your words and what you are vibrating in the sounding of them. That is all important, because you are the creative force. You are changing the vibration of thought into words, therefore the responsibility of how that form is to be created, rests with you. This is not a new thought for you, but I know from my contacts with you how important it is at this point of world evolution that you should become aware of *your* share in the shaping of what life is to become.

We have seen many "come to scoff, but remain to pray". How many full of curiosity, saw and heard and found hard to believe what they saw and heard! What have these years meant in your life? How much have you altered your life so that you truly walk with Him? Personal responsibility and freewill have always been taught, and yet many still seek to make others responsible for their own words and deeds. They are standing in their own way of progress because they will simply not accept personal responsibility. Ease, not peace of mind, and comfort of body have become of paramount importance in this world. Dishonesty in speech, in action, to friends, relatives or employers is treated very lightly, because it is always thought of as being a physical thing. Unless the person is found out it does not seem to matter. What of the sight and hearing of God? I would counsel you to draw a pattern of the fundamentals of your life, and find out exactly, within yourself, what you know your own faults and failings to be. Then cease to look on them either as weakness, fault, or failing. Look straight at your human self with the pure white light of selflessness and then you will see these weaknesses as something you have built on a false foundation.

Let me remind you again of the very well-known words, "Know Thyself"! That must always be the first step towards re-creating the self. To know yourself is not merely to examine your human mind and its reactions. It is also to remember that you have, and can use, three distinct planes of consciousness, the spiritual or super-consciousness, the soul or soul-consciousness and the human consciousness. These three should be blended into one and used constantly in your living.

In the first place, you have, of course, to make very sure that you *truly* desire to change your intensely human outlook on life, and all it means. Are you really willing "to give up all that you have", which means human personality and all its desires, and follow the Master in His Way of life?

This decision is not easily made for it means clearing away a great deal that you hold very dear, much of which, you have told yourself, you cannot do without, or of which you have persuaded yourself, and perhaps others, that *they* cannot do without from you.

You have to face what the Christos faced, the opposition of people who may mean a great deal to you at the moment, the sneers, the scorn which He endured because He would not forsake His chosen path. You will face days, nights and hours when your personality will clamour for the place it so long held. You will have doubts. You will feel hopeless and bereft of all that is dear to you, but through all this, you can be sure of the strong upholding and uplifting of Christ's love—a love that seeks nothing for itself, but gives all—a love that finds its expression in vibrating love, asking for no reward, but knowing full well that love, freely given, will return a thousand-fold stronger.

I know that there are those who put physical and material conditions before their spiritual welfare. There are some who have allowed themselves to be swayed by the desires and opinions of other people. Do not forget that these do not need to be expressed in words or deeds. Their vibrations will reach you. There are those who have acted against the promptings of their inner conscience. There are those who have deliberately built up in their minds, the soothing thought that it was not really *their* fault that they had withdrawn the gifts they had offered to God and His world, though deep down within them they knew they could have overcome the obstacles if they had truly wished, and had sought His help to do so. There are those who, filled with pride of self, have denied the service they could have given if they had overcome or transmuted that pride. There are those who, knowing the gifts as theirs, seek the praise of man in the using of them. To each of these and to all of you who know so well what is holding you back from further evolution on the true Path of Life, but are loath or afraid to admit it, I say, "Let this year be one in which you will use courage to find your weaknesses and endurance in overcoming and transmuting them, strength to continue the fight for truth, purity of thought and deed to cleanse the personal self. These can bring to you the peace that passes all understanding.

We ask that these words may be received in love as they are given.

For Thy servers, O God, we ever pray, that they be fully conscious, day by day, of Thy power within them, and of their power to use it, in the expression of their daily living, whatever form it takes. May they ever seek Thy blessing in all they do and say, for then they cannot be false to Thee. May the power of Thy Spirit, the love and peace of Thy Being, go with Thy children on their many ways. Amen.

CHAPTER 12

ILLUMINATION

As the seasons of the earth change, so do the cycles of man's life. There must ever be, for him, a time of bringing from within, what has grown from the seed of Life, ready to be used in form, in his way of living, in this earth plane. The knowledge of the mind can only contain, what it has the power to draw to itself; but the deeper consciousness, within the Higher Self, is ever able to commune with the Fount of All-Wisdom. Man must learn to draw, from within himself, the Light of Wisdom that will illumine all earthly knowledge and bring him to a fuller, deeper understanding of his own being. The greatest source of help, in this work, will be found in the stillness, the silence of the soul, for it is there, that the seeking soul stores the lessons learned in all planes of Life. When the harmonizing of the self comes into being, that is when the mind is controlled by the purity of the Higher Self, the blending of earth knowledge and spiritual wisdom can take place. Then will come individual inspiration that will guide the soul upon its way.

Do not depend too much on the working of the physical minds, based on physical happenings or people. If you constantly do so, you place obstacles in your own path. Your earthly mind-force can only reach out to the mental planes of this world and so all your arguments and conclusions will be formed, by what your mind receives from these planes. If you surround your life with physical thoughts of yourself and others, you must, by the working of the Law of Vibration, bring to your thoughts the vibrations of those, who have left this earth, but have not progressed beyond where you, yourself, are. You will see from this, that you are not only holding back your own progress, but you are helping to hold back the progress of other souls.

You can illumine earthly knowledge by using Spiritual Wisdom. I ask you to think more deeply, and more forcefully of Illumination, which to you is the lighting up of a place of darkness. It is an unfolding and an enfolding. If you seek illumination mentally, you are vibrating to the higher planes of All-Life. You are calling into being those forces within and around you, that can vibrate to the very centre of Wisdom and fill you to overflowing with the peace which it brings.

Your eyes and your senses are filled with the beauty of fulfilment, in the fruitfulness of growth and production, which is all around you today, and is the result of giving and receiving. Take your lessons from nature. The earth would not be filled with that beauty today if she had not opened herself to receive the life-giving rays of the sun and the moon, for the gifts of God are given to all growing things to use. If you have ever worked in and with the soil, you well know the satisfying of that deep hunger, that lies within you. As your hands work in the soil, the elements of which it is composed, send their vibrations pulsing through you and you give to it, even as you receive from it, in the satisfying of what you can never express in words. You know yourself to be at one with the Creator of all. That, however, does not apply to the earth alone. It can be applied to every way of life. To bring illumination to your life is to grow upwards and outwards but the growth must always start from within.

Man has become increasingly more dependent upon the satisfying of the senses. The use of the hands, the eyes, the brain in the simpler, humbler tasks of life is being put aside and man seeks fulfilment through what others have made, and put into his hands to use. The Creator gave to man the qualities and the powers that he has, so that he would use them to help all growth. In so doing, he would draw into this world the vibratory forces of the Higher Planes. Only by that way of living can true evolution come to pass.

Whatever your path in Life, wherever your work may be, do not be hemmed in, or bound by them. Release yourself! Let light come into action in your life and you will find that all things are changed! The difficulties, the problems, the worries, that your mind conceives, can be broken up by the rays of Light, and they will become clear to you.

Let your mind rest, for a time, in the thought of the life of the Master. He was a creator, as a child, as a boy, as a man. He was not content simply to make or fashion a thing. He would always try to find a way to perfect it. He would never say, "Oh! That must do!" He would look on his work, and then try and find where he could change it, to make it even better than it was. That was the lesson, he sought to teach to those, who walked the earth with Him. He taught them not to dwell on the outer form but to seek and find the inner meaning. What a lot of trouble you would save yourself today, if you, too, sought Illumination in all you do and say. Your course of action would be changed because your outlook would be changed. No longer would your work be done, because of what you got as a result of doing it. You would do the work as a creator, however humble your work might seem to be.

With the talents that God had bestowed on Him, the Master could have taken His place among the highest and most gifted of men. Yet He chose first to perfect the work of His hands. He became a carpenter. He fashioned yokes, and all through His earthly life He used the lessons He had learned in the workshop, to help others. When those around Him were tired and discontented and wanted him to leave the people, spending more of His time with them, giving only to them, He would look at them, say no words, but in that look they knew that the light of His being penetrated the darkness of their minds, to bring them the peace they sought. Yet, He had always taught them that peace must first be created *within* the self. It was useless to seek it in words or teachings; if they were not prepared to make themselves at one with Him and with His teachings. Just as when working in the soil, you gather into yourself all the vibratory forces of the earth, so He taught, that if you make yourself at one with all men, you will give greater service to them all.

You bind yourself with bonds you find hard to loosen. Your way of life is too confining, too enclosed by the lives of others. Break free from the thraldom! Let the light come out, from within you, and shed its rays on all people and on all their ways of life! As it comes from within and as the desire to shed these rays grows stronger, so it will break the bonds that hold you. The difficulty, you find hard to overcome; the hurt that is a constant ache within you, what are they? Are they of your own creating? Whatever may have been the beginning, the cause, you are dealing with the effect. You are shaping *your* life, *your* actions on what your mind has created from it. Let it go! Hold yourself still until you see His light and His love seeking to help you to find the truth. You put *your* meaning into words that are spoken. You see what *you* want to see, as the result of other people's actions; but that *you* is not the Higher self. It is the Personal Self. Can you not set it aside, and seek the greater Light? To you, if you truly seek, Illumination will surely come.

Do you remember how the disciples so often misunderstood what the Christos said, because they would translate all His words by their physical meaning. Yet, He was seeking to bring to them the knowledge of the inner meaning of all things in life.

"Seek and ye shall find!" These are comforting words. Hold them close to your heart, but ever remember the word "Seek". Do not accept and leave it there! Seek, seek, and never cease to seek, that you may find the truth within yourself! It lies deep within you, as deep as a well, and must be sought with a light! Christ came to bring light to the world, and He is still pouring forth the rays of His light into every heart that is open to receive them. But He cannot *open* your heart! He came, and still He comes, not to break laws, but to fulfil laws! That is what you too must seek—the fulfilling of the Law. The Law of Love holds all the principles of life within it; but do not seek to measure Love by an earthly standard. Love, that is the Law, is too vast, too deep, too strong to be held within a physical limitation. Release it, in your own thoughts and deeds, and you will find that your whole life is changed and your strength renewed. No longer will your pathway be dark and steep. No longer will you be surrounded by shadows that obstruct your view. No longer will you be held or bound by this one or that. You will be free, as free as Christ was, because you will have released within you the Creative Power that will bring light to every step you take. You will no longer see your life in terms of days or years. You will see it as an endless path illumined by His love.

What can you find in the earth life that will surpass the surety of His love? It knows no shadowing. It never turns aside. It is in truth, "the love that will not let you go"! What is the reason? It is because, as all pure love, it seeks nothing for itself, for love is a giver. Not only did Christ teach that, but He lived it, all through His life, despite criticisms and condemnations of those He taught. He ever held fast to the selflessness of God's love. His disciples fought among themselves, as to who would be nearest to Him, or who would travel with Him on His journeyings. He called each one to Him, because He knew the point or stage of evolution to which his soul had reached. He also knew that within them lay the power to make their lives anew, and to rise to His call, to go out into all the world and feed his flock. He knew, too, even as He had been tested, they too must be tried and tested, and must prove themselves worthy of the gift of service offered to them. You know that He died upon a cross of wood, but did He not also live upon a cross—a Cross of Service—that brought to Him much suffering? In that suffering, however, was joy, because He knew that it was a preparation for the gathering-in of souls, an opportunity to help in the evolution of the earth world.

At times, He had to watch His servers deny His teachings, and turn again and again, to the satisfying of their self-desires; but, because He knew that this was a part of their growth, He had the strength to go on watching and waiting for that time, when they would truly give up all that they had for His service in the world, when they would give up not only their personal goods, possessions and careers, but also the lower, or less progressed, self and all the gratification it seeks, so that freely and selflessly they would walk the Path of Service.

You will immediately say, "How hard all this sounds!" One can but repeat, as He did, vibrating with All-Love, the sounds of the earth words to help and to strengthen each one in this giving-up. Only when you truly know the self are the gates opened, the bar on the portals of the Higher planes lifted, and you can enter, with Him, into everlasting peace and love.

There is no law that can be applied to all lives, except the Law of which we have spoken, the Law that can only be fulfilled by living it as He did, in thought, in word, and in deed. That is why each one is here, in this plane, because here, today, even as in His day of life, are all the opportunities for fulfilling the Law.

You say that the ways of life are very different now. That is not true! The outer aspect may have changed but you are all here, because you have the power within you to live courageously, and not to be held or bound by any person or desire, but to be free to create not only your way of living, but also, in that way of living, to help all mankind to create anew in life all that is not in keeping with His Law of Love.

The way of living may be different today, but the same opportunities, the same testings are given to you, as were given to His followers. They, too, had to meet the same temptations in earthly ways, through their own desires, and the desires of those around them. They, too, were called selfish and unkind, because they would not follow the usual paths of living in those days. Deep within yourself lies the truth of the self. Continue, then, the seeking and the searching until you find your true being, hard as it may be to walk the path and hear the condemnations of those who watch your actions! Hold ever in your thoughts that you are walking in His steps, while the things of the earth and the people, in your life, may be very dear to you, are they worthy of the price you are paying for them?

Seek first the Kingdom of Love, and all the joys will be created by your own acts, for that is what the Master always taught. "By their fruits shall ye know them!" Till the soil, blend and water it with strength and the waters from His fount of love and your harvest will be golden and your gardens full of beauty!

May the blessing of the ever loving Father, the peace and the love of the Christos be with you, in your seeking. May you ever feel and know His presence in every action in your life, and make of it an offering of love to Him. Then will your life be lived in Illumination, and you will be at one with Him.

Peace be in your heart and in your life. Amen.

CHAPTER 13

BEAUTY

If you would know yourself and progress into the Way of Light then you must know and use the beauty of Life.

Beauty in physical life may be expressed in beauty of thought, of speech and of action and these three, though one, may be used in different ways. You and I are of God. We are all-Spirit. God thought of the beauty of life, and in that thought He created us all. As *He* did, so can you. It is for you to create, in that same form of beauty. It is for you, in your earthly bodies, to use these creative Forces, that you may bring into the density of matter, which you know as the Earth Plane, that Force which will go on its way and return again to its Creator, for all that God has sent forth will return again to Him.

This, your day of life, which is only a small part of the whole day of life, is but a little breathing space upon the Way. You have come this way, that you may use all that you have gathered in the spheres and states through which you have passed. You are Spirit and therefore you are not entirely dependent upon what you find in the earth to nourish and sustain you. A part of you will be sustained by that, which is truly a part of yourself. The elements of your body (air, earth, fire and water) will receive nourishment and sustenance *from* these same elements, which are around the earth planes. Your souls will be nourished by the God Force within these same elements, which you draw within your body to sustain it.

You know the importance of the rays of the sun and the rays of the moon in the physical form of life. No earth form can grow and give forth, without the life-giving and light-giving properties of these two sources. Your body must absorb these rays. It is fed by them and so is your soul. Your spirit does not depend upon these rays for your spirit is a part of the great Source of Life.

Spiritually, you are a creator. What you create with your thoughts, your lips and your hands are not mere manifestations of physical matter or a gathering together of elements in this earth, producing form. It is fundamentally much deeper than that. The true creative force of life is God. Man, by his mind force, and actions of his body may gather together the minerals and elements of the earthly kingdoms and shape them into form, but it cannot be done by action alone. It is the Creative Force which, like a stream flowing down a mountainside, breaking its way through all barriers and absorbing into itself all that is in its path, is the central idea of your being.

It is *that* idea, which is your creative energy. It is *that,* which out of the experience of the soul-matter, the consciousness, rises to the mental body, and is again sent forth in the form of thought, to be brought back in what you know as form. In that form, you have gathered together all the life forces, and it is the Spiritual Forces within them, which you know as energy and atoms, that create that form. Purity of thought is of such importance, in the manifesting of your life today. You cannot expect to find beauty in your world, if you do not produce beauty in your thoughts. You cannot hope to have a world that is truly spiritual, if everything, that is of the Spirit, which is within you, is brought forth in a purely material way. Let us look, for a moment, at the beauty of speech and the beauty of action.

Here in the earth vibration takes the form of light, sound, colour and number. These are vibratory forces, and in the sounding of words, you produce all these vibrations. If you are spiritually gifted, and have used the forces within you to develop these gifts, every sound that is made upon the earth, you could not only hear with your ears, but you would also see the colour produced by that sound. You would see and feel the light, or the shade of it, and you could respond to its number. Speech is so potent a force that comes forth from you, so unheedingly at times, that it is most important to try and convey to the chelas of Esoteric Teachings, the need to be careful in this speech, and to realise more fully, what they are releasing when they speak. Has man not become more animal-like in his sounds? Individuality is being lost. It is being submerged by the personality of those around you! Why is it, that each one, who has the power to express his own self, is continually sounding what he has heard others sound? You listen with your ears, and many times, what you hear jars upon your mind. There is something, within you, that does not like the sounds that are made; and yet, because you want to be like others, because you don't want to feel that you are different in any way, you will actually take into yourselves these vibrations and produce them again. So it goes on and on, in this plane of earth, and the accumulation of sound becomes more and more dense.

As you speak, you produce sound waves, which must work in their own force. They are produced, merely, as physical sounds. If you are only saying what you think will please others, if you are repeating what you have heard others say and if you fashion words, merely, that they will create impressions on the minds of others, then you are producing sound waves, that will continue to sound only as far as their force will carry them. As you have fashioned them out of purely physical desire, and of your physical being, they will continue to work on that vibration. The ethers will receive them and their vibration will go on sounding for all to hear; but the spiritual sounds that you make will pass over them. They will not absorb them. They do not want to do so, for they know that these physical vibrations cannot be of any service.

How wrong it is to waste words and energy! To be able, by God's grace, to produce something, that can travel on and on, eternally giving forth, raising the fallen, strengthening the weak. To neglect to do this, and to produce meaningless sounds is surely wrong! Listen to the sounds, that you produce! Listen, not with the physical ears, to the sounds, that many consider sound well, and whose effect on others affords them such pleasure, but rather listen with the ear of the inner self! Listen to your own vibration, as you pray, today, that peace and love may dwell in the hearts of mankind!

You ask God to help you, but can you not realise that, in vibrating empty, meaningless sounds, you but add to the density of the vibration of the planes of earth? Can you not understand, that you are forming clouds, so dark and so heavy, that only man is able to breathe and live in them. Do you realise, when you use words and phrases, created, perhaps, by others for you, that you are using something which will lower the rate of vibration of all the kingdoms, which, God has said, you should bring to perfection. Do you realise amidst your laughter, amidst your falseness of sound and satisfaction, that you are lowering your own rate of vibration? Ask yourself if it is worth it! In this world, today, so many, anxiously, want their money's worth, and are so beset with the material value of things! They want to be sure, that whatever they give, they receive full value for it in return. If you give in this way you have forgotten the teaching of the Christos. He taught that it was not wise to lay up treasures on earth. If, in your speech, you are sounding vibrations which are filled with the desire to impress others, then you are truly laying up for yourself treasures which may remain only on earth, for these vibrations will not reach even the Astral Spheres. They will remain in the density of this earth which is filled with discord, strife, war, death and destruction.

Those who are dedicated servers of the Master and who have been taught that they are "Bearers of the Light" which is to be used in the ethers of this world to cleanse them, to heighten their vibration and to bring this earth, again, into its true vibration of Light, when the shadows and darkness will disappear as they are brought into this Light, they must ask themselves why they speak as they do. Why are you, Chelas of the Master, so anxious that all your words and phrases, your tones, the intonations of your voices should be so much of one pattern? Why is it, that if you can raise a little laughter at, what you call, your cleverness, you are satisfied? You know, so well, that all you have done is to create a sound vibration, which will remain in that cycle of the earth. Is it not better, that your thoughts should have that beauty, of which I have spoken, so that, in your thoughts, you create the force from which your speech will take its form? You will never be asked to cast from you anything that is full of beauty, joy, happiness or light.

How are you to find beauty and light and the place of God? How are you to use them? Lose the ideals, that you have set for yourself in the physical way of life! Take a few moments of quietness and go over the conversations that you have had with others! You will realise how empty and meaningless was much that was said, how often words were used solely to impress the listener.

How many times do those who are dedicated workers of the Master say, "I must really try and remember that I am a Light-

Bearer, I am Spirit. God has given me a voice and a body, through which to manifest sound, and by doing so, to speak words which will help my fellow-men." Then in the stress and bustle of earthly life, that great desire, to be one among many, comes again, and the beauty of that thought is lost. Hold hard to the beauty of thought! Give to others all that is true within your mind, by using your individuality, and eliminate any desire to create an impression on physical lives! Seek rather to create that which is spiritual in others, by the sound vibrations which you send forth! God sends to all, those sound waves. If He did not you could not produce sound. There is nothing in you, as a physical being, that can create anything. It is the sound of the voice of God, in each one of you, that is your voice. The sounding forth of man, as a physical being, is the work of God. *You* cannot create anything without that Life Force, which is God. While you hesitate to use the name of God in any actual terms, and you probably pride yourself that you would not use unclean language, do you not realise that, if you utter words and phrases which really convey nothing more to your hearers than the fact that you are able to speak as they do, you are creating something that is unclean? Speech is such a beautiful thing. Speech can be a wonderful force of good! If you were to cease to think of yourself in your speech, and think of those to whom you are speaking, I am sure you would be more careful of, and more guarded about, the forces which you send forth. Your sound waves would no longer merely travel through the ethers of these planes, or go circling round them, but they would pass on, in their light ray, into the higher planets and spheres and would increase their strength. As the moisture of the earth is taken up, and returned again in the form of rain to purify and strengthen the forces of the earth, so these sounds that you have created by the power of God within you would again return to the earth plane. They would return with the added strength of your own spiritual spheres. They would be encased in a ray of light, and as they came again into the ethers of the earth plane, they would be able to touch and dispel darkness, transforming it to light. If each one were to sound forth the *Spiritual* desire really to change the vibrations of the earth, a new world would be created!

Many times you ask for help to put these things into action, but it is useless to cry for help, if, when the help comes, you refuse to use it. Likewise, it is useless to ask God for help to do things, for

He has given you, all the forces of your soul and body, through which you use your spirit. When those, in the Spiritual spheres, wish to travel, they use Thought Force. The desire is there, and in that desire they go. So it is with speech. They do not speak as you do, and yet they can produce sound. They make vibrations that can travel through all planes and can come to the Earth plane, bringing their own Spiritual Forces. They can, by lessening that degree that their Spiritual Force may harmonise with the sound waves of the earth, produce through physical throats what you use as sound. Every time you speak, the sound waves, that you produce, will travel to someone. They will go to some part of the earth kingdom. They will go out into the ethers and you will hear, one day, in the great Spheres of Light, those sounds that you have produced. You will see, not in form, but in waves of force, those etheric waves, which would produce those sounds in the lives of other people.

As you move about the earth, from one place to another, you create waves, that is, you are vibrating in your own force. You know that, according to the desirelessness of the Being that is really you, you will create either dense vibrations of your own physical being, or you will create those lighter vibrations of your spirit. Yours is the choice. You have freewill, and so you cannot be made to produce anything. Only true desire will help you to create what will take you along the Path of Light. So often you say, "We have to do such and such a thing, if we want to get on in life!" "To get on in life" is such a stupid phrase! What you really mean, by it, is to succeed materially, in the material planes of life. How far will that take you, if your treasure is laid up on earth only? Surely, when you pass out of your physical body, you will find yourself in the position you have created. You will certainly be satisfied by your desires, but you will find that you are still attached to the earth by reason of these desires!

Often people say, "Why is it, when a person is very good, does the best he can, uses every force that he has at his command to do good, that he suffers so much and very often is deprived of so much? Sometimes, if he had a better position, or more money, he would be able to do so much more."

Here is the answer. Those, whom you find, in the earth are really spiritual, you do not recognise with your physical vibration. You know them within your Higher Self. If they are in deprived conditions, they are there because, at one time, they have had the position and the means to do what they wished to do. Their opportunities were given to them, and they used them rightly. Therefore there is no more need for them to have the great responsibilities of wealth or position.

Everything comes to you because it is right for you. If, for a time, the difficulties of life have been very great and you now find that they have become easier, that you do not need to struggle so much, then you will know that you have reached such conditions, not to give you ease of mind or body, but to give you the opportunity to use that ease rightly or wrongly. To progress, in any way, is always to accept greater responsibility.

Do not think that those who have evolved spiritually are better off than you are. They are not! They have merely accepted responsibility in a different form. Your responsibility and theirs must always be the same. Whatever you are using, be it thought, speech or some gift God has bestowed on you, the responsibility is the same for all, it must be used on its highest vibration, so that all will receive from it the fulness of its force.

And now to Beauty of Action! If you have truly sought to keep beauty in your thought, by not allowing anything impure or unclean to rise or remain in your thoughts for an instant, but ever to keep the aspiration of your spiritual self consciously in your thought forces, then you will soon find that your mode of speech will alter and that you will be less anxious to talk. You will not want to produce sound, in speech form, all the time, and you will be more careful. The beauty of your thought will show in the beauty of your speech, and the beauty of your speech must also find its expression in action. That is the physical way of life. All things in your physical life must be expressed in action, for whatever is created in your mind will come out in form. You may not be able to fashion material articles, but you will think of action, and as you think, so you will create. You may speak of action and again as you speak of it, so you will create it. There is nothing in your life that you do in your mind, or with your body or your senses, which does not require action and it is for you to say, upon all the planes of manifestation, when that action is to take place.

Individuality is what you must aim to express. Out of all the distress of mind or body, out of the troubles and cares that beset you, the World of Spirit is looking towards this race, in the world planes of life, to put into action the Force of the Spirit and all the Forces of Light will bring the strength and the purity to help achieve it!

All action is important in your physical life, if only because of the vibration, which it sets in action, in the World Planes. If action is the outcome of beauty in your thoughts and the desirelessness of self, then we know that for every single thing that is destroyed thousands and thousands will be built up. How well we know the ringing notes of anger, derision, hatred, and of the desire for destruction, that are produced in the Planes of Earth! But they can be caught up in the ethers, into Light, and you and we can transmute them into a power that will re-create what is good, what is of God. No thought of bitterness, no thought of scorn can do that! These thoughts will only forge weapons that will destroy those who thought them! But the power of Light can raise all things and if your thoughts are filled with purity and beauty, and your speech is sending out light vibrations of beauty, that will come into action, those words which you speak will be caught up in the great Force of Light. They will be used to meet those other forces sent out to you that are not good.

When you hear voices raised in anger, when you hear voices raised in condemnation of their fellow creatures, think what is being done! The vibration of the earth world is being lowered and astral matter is being created! Great density is being created in this plane of life, and you must work to use the Force, which God has given you, to counteract this. Would you not like to create something which would live forever? When, in the world, you see beauty and look upon its form, you think of those who produced it, and of how wonderful it must have been to be able to create something at which men and women still look and enjoy. You stand and gaze at a beautiful building or painting. You listen to beautiful music, you hear sounds of words strung together which touch something within you which is undefinable and you think, "If only I could do that, speak words, sound notes or play something that, in years to come, men and women would still be able to gaze upon and see and feel its beauty!" Well! go out and do it. There exists no reason why you should not!

Is there any one of you who has not been touched by the note of a bird? Have you ever, perhaps when worried, depressed or ill, listened to those clear notes sounding forth in the ethers, and not felt a chord within you sound in harmony? Of course you have, every one of you. That is what each one should be doing in the world today. The beauty of your thoughts, the beauty of your speech, the beauty of your action should be like these spontaneous notes of the birds, going out at all times, knowing well that nothing can destroy them, for beauty can never be destroyed. Beauty in form, yes, that can be destroyed. God is beauty. God has never created anything that is not lovely. Everything that He has ever thought is beauty.

Many sounds of the earth are as the beating of empty drums. They are noise, din and clamour! There is no beauty in them. Remember, in your lives, that the most important thing is contained in that one word, beauty, for that is God! If there is beauty in thought, in speech and in the action of your physical lives, then peace will be within you and around you and God's blessing will be upon you. Where there was darkness, there will be light. Where there was weakness there will be strength and for weariness there will be rest.

Chapter 14

INTUITION

We speak many times of a "Gift from God". Many are the gifts that God has given you, not only personally, but of this world and all that it contains!

You know how emanations and vibrations from you, can affect all and everything, wherever they may be, in this, or other Planes of Life: but think, not only of what you are giving, but also of what you are receiving. Every part of all worlds is a living force vibrating the God Force, each according to its own degree of progression and its desire to do so. Vibrations and Emanations of Force do not belong solely to the human kingdom. They are of all kingdoms, but of all these kingdoms, the Great Spirit has chosen to give to the human kingdom a Divine Consciousness, which can use the wisdom of the Spirit, which the soul has brought with it to this human plane. This is intuition.

How much, in your daily life and work, do you use your intuition? How much, or how little do you know of your ability to use it? Man has become so dependent on his physical powers that, in this present age, he has an ever-increasing desire to express his force in physical and material ways, with the result that he is becoming more and more attuned to the physical expressions of his outer or personal self. Seek to find the true self, for you still discuss and question, with each other, your actions and your thoughts! Would it not add to the growth of your progressing soul, if you sought the explanation of your thoughts and actions, within yourself?

"Be still and know that I am God" are good words that you would do well to remember, when you find your lips producing many, other than good, sounds! How still can you be? For how much of your time are you content to be alone, ALL ONE, which is when the Spirit, the Soul and the Body truly blend into one? Do you find that, when no-one else is present, your thoughts turn to words in your mind? That is the process of bringing *out* thoughts, not of going deeper, within. You say that is hard to do. You think that if you do not understand something, it is better to seek counsel or advice from others and hear their thoughts about it. Would it not be better to learn from the wisdom of the Spirit within you? This you can only do when you have learned to be still, to question your mind thoughts, so that the Force of the All-mind Force may flow to your physical mind and you will know.

How often do you take certain ways, speak certain words, or perform some deed, only to feel, very soon afterwards, that it was not a good thing to do, or say? Why? It was because you followed the reasoning of your human mind that can only function according to the training it has received.

If you were to study more closely the ways of the Beloved Christos when on earth, you would find that much of the suffering He endured was caused through following His own Spiritual Way. Those who followed Him often said, "It would have been better, had He done this or that", but they, as you, had only used their earthly mind and so could not see by the true light, the cause behind the effect.

One of the greatest gifts of the Great Spirit to man is the power to use freewill, to go beyond the limitation of man-made rules of living, and to follow the directions He gave to all mankind.

In your turn, *you* can give to mankind the gift of what you bring from the inner self, to vibrate to all who live. This is the gift of God, which you have within you; but what of those gifts outside yourself? How much do you know of the *things* around you, not just of the *people* you meet, but of the things you use and of everything upon which your eyes rest? How much real use do you, who live in towns and cities, make of the Earth Forces—the trees, the growing things, the flowers? Do you, as you see them, think of your at-one-ness with them, remembering that the God Force, that flows through you, flows also through them? Do you think of your food not just as daily bread, or even as something necessary or pleasing to your body, but as an essence from the source of Life, that is giving itself in service to you, so that, with you, it can emanate its gift again to God. Just as the buds, left when the old leaves have fallen from the trees, will again burst into new leaf through and by the power of the gift of Life and will blend with the elements of earth, air, sun, rain, wind, frost and snow to produce again the beauty of a tree in full bloom, you, too, should be using your daily bread as a truly spiritual gift.

How many of you are missing opportunities of extending the experiences of your soul? By being blind and deaf to the gifts of God around you, and by filling your mind with sights and sounds and thoughts that are of no real help, you are not progressing in the true way of living. Wherever you are, whatever you are doing, you can train yourself to think unconsciously, by not allowing your mind to put your thoughts into words.

You do not consciously think of what is taking place in your bodies, or why you can walk, talk, see, hear, touch or use any of your senses. You just *do* these things. Why then, do you not seek to use the Power of the Spirit of Life in the same way, in all your way of living? Talk less and *be* more!

Work is so limited in its service, because so many hold it in its limitation of the human brain. Do you make an act of service each day? Do you live to give or to receive?

"I am with you in all your ways," said the Beloved One. He is with you, not only when you are in a consecrated place, or in the quiet of your home, or shut away from your fellow creatures in your search for stillness and quietude. He was always seeking an active giving. Well He knew and taught to all the source and force of Life and while His teachings have lived on, in words, into which man has put his own meaning, He gave of the very source of His being to all. He could never separate Himself from any life, and that is why His work still goes on upon the earth today.

You do things that you should not because you measure your life, and all it holds, by physical and material rules and laws. Your great wish is to satisfy your own interests, even although, often, it means the delaying of your own or another's soul progress. How often does this ever occur to you? The opportunity is with *you.*

Think not so much of the self and its progression; but think of the evolution of the world, for which each one shares the responsibility.

Many times, there is sorrow and a retrograde step on the path of progress when a soul follows the desires of self. In that retrogression the soul draws others with it.

The Master asked of the Great White Spirit that He might touch your heart, so that it might be filled to overflowing with His love. Remember, you who are a Chela, that His love and His wisdom are not as physical love and wisdom which give and take as they so desire. Love, that is Wisdom, acts according to the promptings of the inner self, not the outer self. To be of service, in the progression of the soul, to help to draw another nearer to the God-Force, may often come from what appears to be a withholding, and yet that is the true giving of the real self.

Weigh all your actions by the standard of the Spirit of the Christos, and, in His light, you will not be found wanting! He will ever strengthen you upon your way. Be filled with His love-wisdom, that as you go your way, you may be filled with the courage that *is* love-wisdom! Have no other God but Him, who gave you life, that you may give to Him, as He freely gives to you!

CHAPTER 15

THE GREAT EASTERTIDE

At the season of Eastertide, when all around there is evidence of the renewal of all living, growing things, the promise was given. "Behold I make all things new"—the promise of fulfilment. This was not confined to the One who spoke these words. You, too, in your lives, are ever being called upon to renew the Forces of Life, in your mind, in your soul and in your body, and in so doing, to give, through them, the vibrations necessary to renew the Spiritual Forces in others.

That Force, which you call nature, is giving to you now, in your earth, the manifestation of the Law, that Power is used in growth, and development. It is proving to you that darkness and difficulty cannot prevent the Power of the Spirit from doing its work. The trees, the grass, the flowers, all show to you how the strength can be taken in and used to make things new. In your life too, you can use all the adversities and trials that come to you. They can be brought into the Light and used in service. When you see this in your own life in that aspect, you, too, will make all things new.

The Beloved Master passed through deep waters to be tested in His love for His Father and for all mankind. This was ever the Way of Testing. In spite of scorn, of the misunderstanding of His actions and words, never did He change His ways, nor fail in the fulfilling of the Law. The Law that teaches that aspect is Balance. In all the Ways of Life Balance must be used mentally and physically. Emotional forces are the enemies of balance. So, as in nature, you must learn to use everything with which you come into contact, to help you to understand balance. You must learn to balance your emotions with your Spiritual Force of Will, so that there will pour into your mental body that vibratory aspect of the Law of Balance, which will ever give you strength to act in the right way.

When I speak to you, Chelas, of the *right way,* I mean, *The* Way, where all things are blended into the great Eternal Force, that is the source of life. You cannot take to yourself the credit for what *you* make of your life, for, if the personal self were to have its way it would seek expression only on its own plane. Here again, you must bring balance into action. You must blend the personal into the impersonal, and so come into harmony with the Law.

The Christos said He came not to destroy but to fulfil. By using balance you do *not* destroy. You lift up conditions into the impersonal, or Higher Vibration of Spirit. There alone can they find their true expression.

Upon the earth, there is much talk of the sorrow and suffering of Jesus the Christos. It would be better if you, in your thoughts, would dwell on the inner joy of His Being, in the fulfilment of His purpose—to the body, suffering; to the Spirit, joy.

Many talk of the difficulties of life, of the uncertainty of the future, but there is not enough talk of the opportunities which are brought to each one, day by day, nor of the sure promise, that in the future, he will reap what he has sown. That is something you should hold in your mind, for only you can sow the seeds in your own living. If you allow others to do so, that is your responsibility. We teach personal responsibility and the use of Freewill, which the Father has given to you. It is of as little purpose to try and make others responsible for what *you* are, and for what *you* do, as it is wrong for others to try and imprint *their* ways into *your* way of life, and deprive you of your own Freewill.

Many will not agree with this. Many, too, have barred their Way of Service, because they have allowed others to impose *their* wills, *their* likes and *their* views upon them. Well do we know that these impositions are used as an excuse for not using your own Freewill.

"I ought to do it," you say. "I am expected to do it. I have no right to cause unhappiness or sorrow in anyone's life, because of what *I* want to do." Are you quite sure of that? If that unhappiness or sorrow is brought about by anyone seeking to impose his will on yours, what can he expect?

If you break the Law, you cannot hope for harmony and peace in your life. So often, if you had the courage to go deep within yourself, you would find that you submit to these things because it makes your life easier and more pleasant, but you are only pushing away something that, one day in some path of life, you will have to face and with which you will have to deal. That is where another part of the Law comes into action. As soon as you begin to use your inner strength to face some action, or thought of your own, that you feel is not right, and you seek to transmute it, whatever the physical result may be, you will put yourself into harmony with the Law of Compensation. This cannot fail to bring something to your life for your acceptance. This will bring to you a far deeper peace than any satisfying of your own, or other people's emotions can ever do.

Do not hold in your mind, at this season, the physical suffering of the Beloved One, but rejoice rather in the thought of His great endurance, His undying love, His unfailing strength, which He used in those hours, because *He* had fulfilled the Law. He gave up His body, His life here on earth, that He might prove forever how the Law could be fulfilled, that death is but the door that opens the gateway to a fuller, higher life, where, if you have prepared yourself, you are freed from so many limitations which bind you here.

At this time in the earth, the seeds, which will provide the harvest of fruit, of flowers, of grain, are being sown; but that could not be if the seeds were not fed and cared for by the Great Sower. He alone can bring the harvest. So must it ever be, in *your* life. It is no use to think how great, how wonderful, how clever you are, and to promise yourself what you are going to be or do, if you do not use the powers that the Great Spirit has given to you. The true unfolding of His gifts, without Spiritual Force and Power, cannot be accomplished and yours is the responsibility!

The Christos came to live in the earth that he might teach men and women, by the example of *His* own Way of Life, how *they* could live, blending their Spiritual Forces into every physical thought or deed. He was fearless, because He lived in the perfection of His Father's love. So, too, He has shown to you, by *His* life, all the Forces in action in a human life, and how all the Forces and Emotions must be controlled by the Higher Self, for that is how you succeed in the mastery of self and so come to the Way of Attainment. You must all learn to live by your own strength, for it is inexhaustible. The more you use the real strength of your Higher Self, the greater will that strength be to you! That, again, is the Law, and a part of the cycle of your life. As you pass from the weakness of the self to the strength of the True Self, you pass, all unknowingly, to a higher cycle and a quickened force of vibration. In this condition, the Law of Vibration will operate. When you bring into your living the working of the Laws of Vibration and Balance, you will find that many things, in your living, which you have not been able to understand, will become clear to you. Not only will that happen, but your whole outlook on life will be very different.

You will realise, more fully, your sense of responsibility in an earth life and it will no longer make you fearful, puzzled or unable to deal with as you want. You will take your personal difficulties into the Light, which is another way of saying you will bring the Laws of Vibration and Balance into all you think or do, and you will find that your vision will become clearer, and your thoughts will no longer be clouded with the vibrations from the lower self.

You are in the world to make progress. In your worldly ways of living, when you desire to overcome difficulties, you seek to learn more of the work you are doing. You want to become good, even perfect in it, and to do this you have to bring your mind, your intellect and your knowledge into that work, and apply them to what you are doing. Then you make a success of it; but that method is limiting your work and your life to the ways of earth. If, in using your Mind Force in material ways, you widen your spheres of thought and action and recognise that all you do, in this world, is linking up with the doing of it in the life beyond this earth, then you are really using powers that are not of your physical self, but of your Inner Self and Consciousness. Life will become, for you, a richer, fuller thing. Then you will begin to find your true self and acquire real knowing. This should be applied in all your ways of living, in your work, in your family life, in your friendships, in your business activities, in your home-life. There is no part of your life that you can live fully, and have its richest blessings, unless you use these Aspects of the Law.

To use Balance is important. As in a matter of physical and material importance, you have to think and weigh up the importance of the problem before you can reach any decision about it, so, when you progress and balance your earthly and spiritual qualities, you will find how much wider and clearer your understanding has become. You will no longer want to know how to get the best *out* of life, but how you may put the best *into* life. Light will have come out of darkness, all problems will have become clearer and doubts of self and of others will have gone. Though many times you may retire from the struggle, at least you will have put into action in your life a part of the Law, and one day, when the opportunity comes, you will be able to use the Law more fully. Each time that you do so, the Force will become stronger, until the day dawns when, as you look into your conditions with a balanced mind, that is, when you bring the Law of Balance into your thoughts, then will come, at once, the Force of Vibration that will enable you to put balance into action. The weakness which, so often, drags you back to your old mistakes and faults, will be strengthened. You will cease to doubt your capabilities to make your own decisions. You will cast out fear, as the Christos did, and hold fast to perfect Love.

In your loving of each other, when you hold fast to His Love, jealousy or possessiveness must be absorbed, for His Love is perfect love which knows no limitations and seeks nothing for itself. As He gave, so *you* can give all, with no thought clouding that giving. There will be only a peaceful out-flowing, from you, of strength and peace.

You, who are still struggling within yourselves over those conditions in your lives, can you not make the Eastertide your own? Can you not truly bring all of yourself to the Light and, in the perfect love of the Father and of the Christos, come down from that cross of crucifixion of the self, and rise to a new living? We speak of opportunities that are around you. Before you are the gates of opportunity, yet you will not stretch forth your hands to open them. It is fear, alone, that holds you back, fear of self, and fear of others. What have you to fear? Has the Christos not shown you how to give your love, and yet not be bound by desire? Has He not taught you to give and yet not to ask for anything in return, never to measure the gift, nor to expect any return for it, but, in using the Aspects of the Law of Love, to bring balance to your mind, to your emotional body, and so make all things new? What joy! What peace will be yours! There will be no more struggling with the self! Your life will have become balanced and therefore full of the true Law of Vibration. There will be no more torture and agony of mind, but the sure certainty that the Father's love encompasses you, for now you will have the gift of clear seeing, which, as you use it, will develop your intuition.

Your life and actions are measured by the progress of your soul. God knows what you truly *can* do, but He is not responsible for what you do do, for that is your responsibility. How quickly God and all His helpers are blamed if, by not using to the full the gifts He has bestowed upon you, results are not as you would wish!

You often say, "If I want anything strongly enough, and it is good for me to have it, it will be given to me." That is quite true, but you do not always want what is good, not only for yourself, but good also for your evolution as part of a whole.

So often, by your own actions, you put obstacles in the way of fulfilment. You limit creation by desire and it does not come as you desire it. It would be well if, before accusing the Higher Forces of Light of false words, you were to examine your own thoughts and actions, to find out whether you have used balance in your living and allowed the vibratory forces of selflessness to vibrate through your desires. You will, indeed, make all things new when you do this. Clear your mind of limitations! Put yourself into the current of His love! You will then find your will blending into the infinite will of the Father, who is all love. This must bring to you that peace which passes all the understanding of the human mind.

Chapter 16

THE WORK OF THE DEVAS

I should like, very briefly, to give to you a clearer conception of the Devas and their work on, and in, the Planes of the Earth. It is necessary that you should have a full and deep realisation of how you can co-operate with them, for your life, your earthly life, is really built up of Devic Essence.

The Devas are the very personification of all energy, and of every form, manifested on these planes. You are not conscious of their emanations, but you must remember that you are not really conscious, in the physical sense, of your own or other people's emanations.

You may have conscious feelings about people and places but that is not the same thing. An emanation is a force, which you cannot feel with your physical senses, but only by your sensitivity. So, you must try to heighten your sensitivity, that you may have a deeper awarness, or knowing, of the Inner Forces of all forms of life. When you see, feel or recognise beauty in any form you must train your mind to go beyond the physical feeling that it brings and to reach the source of it. This is not a difficult thing to do, but increasing your sensitivity is not something you can do now and again. It must be a continuous process. If it is not, you create barriers to your own progress.

Spirituality should be an active part of your life, a consciously un-conscious force, which you bring into every thought or deed in your life.

Remember! It is always the motive that counts. How often is that teaching misconstrued! It is such an easy thing for the human mind to create the thought of the good motive, but the true disciple is never satisfied with what is, merely, a thought. He will always seek the true cause of an action. It is, in doing this, that you become more in harmony with the Devic Forces, for you have put yourself into closer contact with them, and opened yourself to receive the out-flowing of their Essence of Life.

You must constantly remind yourself that you are a creator. You are an active creative force, here and now, in this Earth Plane, and it rests with you, and only you, what quality that creative force will have.

If your motive is to create good, you will have no more trouble in deciding whether what you are doing is right or wrong. You will know that if you have cut away the limitations created by physical self-desire, if you have broken away from the limitations which the lives of others seek to set around you, then your motive must be in harmony with the will of the Father-Mother of all life that knows no limitations.

The language of the Devas is vibration, a part, as you well know, of the Law; but it is not a physical vibration, purely of the senses. Sound and colour are of the greatest importance in their work, for these are vibratory forces. Certain colour vibrations can be and are good and helpful in your life, yet, despite the teachings given on this, so often that knowledge is set aside and a colour, or colours that are pleasing to your senses, or help you to follow a certain trend, are used. You can give very real help to the Devas, or Lords of Being, in their work, by using vibrations of colours that are in harmony with your own soul force. By so doing, you become also more in harmony with them.

The balance of the world is constantly being upset by the desires of men and women. In the ethers, the Devas are striving to bring into being, through those who have an understanding of the Inner Teachings of Life, the correct vibratory forces, which you recognise as colour, that the true balance may be restored. So often in this you can prove to yourself how strong or how weak you are, in gratifying your senses or in using your own creative force. In speech, too, remember that, as beings who have sought to learn the inner meaning of All-Life, you are responsible for the creation of sound, brought from Force into Form! If you were to keep that thought, consciously, in your physical mind your speech would not be so slip-shod and you would be more careful of utterances or soundings in your life. You would not, for instance, keep on repeating what you well know are distortions of sound. This is one way to upset the true balance of your own self. To pattern *your* life on someone else's is to deny your self the opportunity to create in true form. In so doing you refuse your service to those Beings, whose work, in these Planes, is to add *their* Higher Forces to yours, through the manifestation of what are called Nature Forms.

The Earth World is showing at every turn what the Creative Force is, and how it produces itself. Would that you could draw it more deeply into your souls, and there let it re-create what you are manifesting in your lives. Think, as you look at the trees, flowers, grass, grain, fruit and vegetables, of what has made them as they are! Think, also, of what has gone into the making of them! I do not want you to think of those who planted, tended and cared for them, but I do want you to think of how the colour, form and contents of these things have been produced. Where is the source of their being? The answer is in the ethers of the earth. The Devas bring into the world the Cosmic Energy, that is the very source of all that becomes Form; but they must use the vibratory forces, acting in the earth, to keep them in the creation of form, and you are in the earth to help in supplying these vibratory forces to them. The tone of your voice, as it produces sound, the quality, or depth of sincerity in the words you speak, the degree of truth in what you say or do, these are all helpful, or otherwise, in the production of any Form.

I know that you will say that it is impossible to think of all that, all of the time. I quite agree with you. Think of it! Be conscious of it, that it may become as much a part of your life, as breathing is an act performed without any conscious forming of thought!

The greatest trouble is that you think with your brains, which immediately brings all your higher aspirations down to a lower plane of physical manifestation. To control the mind you must learn, if you are to give the perfect service we seek to give through you, not to keep spiritual truths on an earthly level, but to bring the earthly way into the Higher Force, where it can be used at all times, and in ways of which your mind cannot conceive. If you learn to control the mind, then a great out-pouring of spiritual energy will come from the Devic forces to you, so that the Devas may blend harmoniously with your ways of living.

If you were to give as much whole-hearted service to us, who seek your help in manifesting the will of the Father in the world, as you do to those in whose earthly service you are, or to the satisfying of your own desires, how different your world would be.

The harmony of the Spheres is what we are all seeking to bring into the earth planes today, for a great struggle is going on in the world, and you are all taking an active part in it, though you may not be conscious of so doing. I, as a messenger of Light and Truth, ask you to join with us in seeking to bring to its true state the balance of your world. Do not help to overthrow it, by withholding the gifts that God has given you, the gifts of creative action in your lives. You will not have to seek long for the outlet. The way lies all around you. Your world is full of people who are sick in soul, mind and body. You can all take an active part in serving, by living your lives in accordance with the selflessness of your soul's desire. You can truly be the builders of the New Age, but you will never build it until you have the courage to listen to the call, "Follow me!" When you emerge and rise above your state of self-immersion and give of your service, freely and willingly, with no thought of anything but the giving, then your emanations will create the Form, which the Devas are seeking to supply with Force.

Self-examination is an excellent thing, but it can be carried too far, for it remains in the physical plane of thought. It must become clear perception and knowing—not thinking. These are the vibrations the Devas are seeking, in which to build colour, sound, beauty and harmony. You, each one, can supply them. You would not, willingly, withhold material help which you could give to those in real need, why then do you deny to your Father that service which He seeks from you, and for which He has endowed you with the necessary material?

"I have need of all my workers." These words, uttered many years ago, and sounded in the earth plane, are still true today. Listen to that cry! Listen, every day of your life and know that you are a worker! Do not question how, or in what way you can serve! Your inner self will bring that to your physical knowledge, if you can put aside the physical restrictions you have made, to prevent that service from being put into action. The humblest task, the simplest word, the kindly action, the selflessness of your giving, those are what count, not the fulfilling of *your* ambitions, or the carrying out of *your* desires. By saying truly and meaning truly, "Not *my* will but *Thine* be done", you will become a true server and a power for good, in your world. The Devas will respond to the note that you sound in the inner worlds. That is why you are taught that it is the motive that counts! It is the motive that is the note. The sounding of it immediately draws a response from those who are in harmony with that sounding. You and they become one in your creative forces; your note will blend in harmony. If that note be of the self, it will create discord, and will not be used by the Higher Forces. It will descend to its own level, and you will attract those lower forces into your own life.

In many varied ways, the Christ taught the control of the self. When you control self, you rise to the higher reaches of this plane and all your senses, emotions and desires are purified.

To understand and control your various bodies is the road to God. To love and serve is the bridge that leads to God.

"Beloved children of the Light, ye come again unto Thy Lord, to blend with those, whose joy it is to touch thee, in this Love. Hold thou thy Life in Love Divine, and thou shalt draw within thee, that which is of Him. Each one is called to give himself as a Bearer of His Light upon the earth, and now thou enterest upon thy Way. Trials and testings will be given. Thy greatest days, on earth, are those wherein thy faith is tested and tried. He walks with thee upon that Way, and when His voice to mortal ear is stilled, and it would seem that thou art alone, call forth the strength which in the hours of dawn has come to thee, and use it in thy daily life.

To each will come, as days go by, the choice between the things of earth and those of Spirit. In that day, you will have need of all your strength, for those, whom you love upon this plane, will not have understanding of your choice. Hold it in thy mind, that in your choice, many will rise or fall.

Great is the knowledge! Great is the responsibility thou bearest, but He, who knows all, will send to thee the Light of Understanding in that hour, so will thy choice be made!

Oh, my beloved children, go forth to do this Work, to make anew those lives upon this earth, that His great purpose may be fulfilled and that Peace and Love may be, once again, the portion of all men!"

Chapter 17

OUTLINE OF DIVINE HEALING
or
THE LAYING ON OF HANDS

Before you can understand Divine Healing, you have to ask yourselves and truly know what is Man? Is he a thing of flesh only and, like a puppet, to be dangled at the hand of fate, or is he something more?

He is, first and foremost, a Spiritual Being, made in the Image of God. He consists of Spirit, Soul and Body and I put them in that order as being the order of importance. The Spirit, which is of God, is immortal and perfect. The Soul, which is the clothing of the Spirit of God, is also part of the Spiritual self, and is better known as The Etheric Body. This is the part of us which lives on, when it no longer has any use for the physical body, or the mortal part of us.

The Soul is the part of us that is seeking evolution or progress, because it brings its imperfections into being in order to try during the earth life to correct these and so progress further along the path of evolution.

We may be unaware of this and we may not realise that the whole world, including ourselves, is a mass of Vibratory Force. Further, man cannot separate his vibratory force from all the kingdoms of the earth, His body, a mass of cells, works, moves and vibrates in Harmony with these Kingdoms, i.e. the mineral, vegetable and animal kingdoms. If not, the cell foundations alter, the shape becomes distorted, and dis-ease and illness, many times with pain and suffering, happen because the Harmony of that has gone. We do not have far to look for these causes, for there are many. Food poisoned by chemical manures, sprays, adulterations of all kinds and the manner in which it is grown. Pollution of the air, noise and destructive vibrations, thought forces released by man and his way of living, his soundings in life, all combine to create harmony or inharmony. Since everything as I have said before is a gigantic vibratory force and we a part of it, it follows that all we do, think and say must affect all with which we come into contact, all that we touch and handle or even brush against. Our footsteps on the pavements leave for others, either helpful or unhelpful, vibrations in which to tread. The preparing of food for our families—give to them either good, love and strength or whatever vibratory forces are within our minds, be it for good or not good. One will build, the other will break down and destroy, and this is our responsibility, for God has given to us His great gift of Freewill.

A poet once said, "I am a part of all that I have met." How true this is, although we often fail to realise it. Do we ever think, for instance, that we *are* a part of every contact that we make, and that the experience appears upon the mirror of our consciousness?

Invisible though it is to the majority of people, each of us has an aura which radiates from and around the physical body, and of which the colour, size and quality can be seen by those with the vision to see. Not always a very pleasant experience, for all emotions are registered within this aura; it is useless to speak words with the lips that deny what is registered in the aura. Again, if disease is present in the body, there is a drooping of the auric force at that point and this can be of great help to one who can see with the vision of Spirit in the diagnosis of disease. If and when the disease or inharmony has been treated and again becomes harmony, the aura at this point will resume its normal shape and size.

Freewill is the greatest gift that God has given to man. He can think and do as he likes. If he breaks a physical or a Spiritual law, then he suffers, and his mind and body do not live in harmony but in inharmony causing disease. He suffers pain, but pain and suffering are not the Will of God for him but something he has caused himself. Very often he finds that all the medical skill does not alleviate or cure; something prompts him to seek further. Has He not said "Seek and ye shall find"?

From the very earliest of time, Divine Healing has always been available to man. Through the centuries it became associated with witchcraft and people used it as a source of power over others.

Consequently at the Convention of Constantinople in A.D. 550, the Church, which up to this time had taught both Karma, or the Law of Cause and Effect, and practised the Laying on of Hands for the purpose of Healing the Sick, discarded these teachings and practices.

Karma, or the Law of Cause and Effect, which is always in action, cannot be disassociated with the Healing of the Mind and Body. There are few who have not, at some time or another, experienced illness, disease, and pain. Many have received the Laying on of Hands or Divine Healing and proved its worth both to the Mind and Body. What is this Force, this Power than can heal, that can remove dis-ease, and make anew cells of man's body? Is it not the Power of God in action? No one can claim this power, though many do, for it comes from God alone, but man can offer himself as a channel or Instrument, in the Hands of God as a channel, for the pouring forth of this Power.

What does this entail then for the one who desires to be used by God in this way? It requires clean minds and bodies that are kept in such a condition that they can be used whenever necessary. It is no use for one who so offers himself, to delude himself that he can live and think anyhow and then be used by the God Force for His Love and Power to be passed through that body to others. Such is as you see a tremendous responsibility and not to be entered upon lightly.

I have heard people say that they have the Power to Heal! Have they? That power belongs to God and not to them. They cannot at will give healing to others, unless God wills. Therefore, they, of themselves have no power. To offer a clean vessel or body, for His use, demands of those who would give this Service, courage, self discipline and a rigorous training of thought and mind forces. Above all, it is essential to have complete faith in God and His Works, and a lack of fear, which proves a great stumbling block to many. Only the use of Love can give the perfect Instrument and like the Surgeon who cannot operate unless he uses clean, sharp and perfect instruments, so must the Server of God be as clean and perfect, that the full flow can pass through him.

Through Love can be poured the Rays and Forces capable of restoring to health and harmony again that which has been diseased and inharmonious. You work very hard to physically obtain the qualifications necessary to obtain a good job with excellent remuneration, but when it comes to Spiritual Gifts, man expects them to be given to him without any effort on his part at all! Why? You will have to work extremely hard if you want to attain Spirituality, or you will not succeed, for only by constant hard work will you be able to learn and attain. Only by living truth, living love, and when I say living I mean just that, will you gain the Spiritual requirements necessary to heal the sick.

Again, do not think that because you are used in this way, that you have finished your work and accomplished much.

You must put into action every day the teachings and the truths of life, as portrayed by the Man Jesus when He walked the earth. This will not be easy. He, with all His Wisdom, did not find it so, so why should anyone of lesser degree hope to find it so. God's gifts are too precious to be handled by those who do not know their true value. How then does this Force work you ask? Just as in this world we have a vast organisation of workers, some in exalted positions, others in lesser ones, so in the World of Spirit there is a still more wonderful organisation.

All Rays and Forces come direct from the Christ Sphere. They are guided and passed on by many Workers, until they reach the Instrument in the Plane of Earth who has given himself in Service to God. During development and long after the Rays have been passed through the Healer, there is a constant testing of the degree of Ray that can be used, also combinations of Rays, which are very numerous. How, in the human body, are they passed?

In the Etheric or Soul Body there are what are called "Centres" or "Chakras" through which these Rays and Forces are passed and although quite different in character and appearance are vibratory forces of varying degree, which are filtered through these "Centres" or "Chakras" by Workers in Spirit to the body of the patient. Unless the Healer lives in accordance with Spiritual Laws, then the strength of these Rays cannot be passed through him and no amount of pleading or desire on his part can remedy this. Only by constant adherence to the Law, by good living and constructive thought, using Love at every turn and being ready to give Service, perhaps at most inconvenient times, can he serve. He cannot and must not qualify his Service to God. How can you get a clear light through a dirty vessel? Neither can the Force of God be used through a Healer if he does not keep his vessel, mind and body, clean and pure.

For one who is dedicated and consecrated to this Work, there is much preparation. Some come to earth specifically to give Service in this way and are prepared before they enter the Earth Belt. Special atomic structure is used and brought into being, with the result that he is very highly sensitised, but even so, is highly subjected, even as Jesus the Man was, to all earthly trials and testings. If he fails the results are tragic indeed.

Others come into this Work through illness or through contacting another who is already a Healer or Worker. Gradually they become aware of potentialities and eventually the day comes when the Soul desires to give its own Service to God in this specified manner. When that happens, I quote "when the pupil is ready, the Teacher is found". So contact is made.

When the Worker has made the dedication of his own soul and found his Teacher, who will guide him towards fulfilment, a conscious effort is made to use the help that is given. Those who, in Spirit, desire to work through that Instrument or Healer gradually draw near, the "Centres" or "Chakras" are gradually opened by them to accommodate the Rays, which are tested and adjusted. No two Healers are used in exactly the same way or for the same degree of Ray or intensity. Sometimes a combination of Rays is used. They are passed Spirally through these centres and not in straight lines as many people think.

Let us now come to the Rays—they are brilliant in colour, scintillating with Light, beyond any depth of colour of which we can think physically. Forces are different, and are banks of colour and are used for very different purposes. Compared with these, the colours of the physical world are completely dull, drab and uninteresting, yet colour vibrations should be used and should play a large part in our physical living.

To use colours that are helpful to the growth of the Soul is a great advantage to the individual. That does not mean that the colours we call "favourites" are always the best ones for us to use. Colour helps the growth of the soul, for remember also that all colour has sound and *vice versa.*

I have known people who, because they have been told that blue, mauve and purple are "Spiritual" colours, dress themselves in these colours and set them around them with the result that there is no harmonisation with the auric forces, or with the growing soul. They have served to draw strength *from* the individual, instead of feeding strength *to* the Soul, to use in its process of evolution.

It is all the more astounding when one sees Chelas who have been taught and who know the teaching on Colour Vibration using colours that they know within themselves are detrimental to them, and find them refusing to use those colours that could help to bring calmness, strength of purpose and growth to them.

It is important then to use the colours to which we vibrate in the Soul Force and not always those that we perhaps like as fashionable or appeal to our senses, or because we think that they are Spiritual in essence! Let us look briefly at some of the colours used.

GREEN: The highest vibratory colour force of the Earth. The colour of growth and creativity. It is cool and calming in its effect and is good therefore for nervous and highly strung people to use and have about them. They, funnily enough, often prefer red, and then wonder why they are irritable and bad tempered!

The green Rays of Healing may be the type that soothe, or they may be "Burning Rays" that are very powerful indeed in breaking down disease of the body. This colour in its pale shades is used for many people, instead of blue, because they re-act more readily to that particular Force.

RED in the material sense is a strong physical colour and we use it to denote danger—the red flag, red traffic light, red lights on roads, etc., etc.

It can be a source of irritation to many people with sensitive nerves and can immerse one completely in physical thoughts and desires, and people who suffer from bad temper would be well advised to avoid using any red shades whatever in their lives.

That is the physical red, but the Spiritual Ray of Red vitalises and brings strong constructive elements to the blood stream and builds and strengthens, but there are certain types of people on whom it would never be used, unless it were the very deep red, the colour of a deep red rose.

ORANGE. A vital part of the Red Ray is the true Life Force and can only be used in moderation. Physically, it is very overpowering, but it stimulates where necessary and is, of course, a wonderfully vitalising power to the whole body. Lesser shades of this colour such as

YELLOW sustain and strengthen the Soul Force and feeds the desire to grow and progress spiritually.

GOLD. This ray is used to bind broken ends of nerves, holds disease in check, re-vitalises the blood stream and organs of the body, lightens heavy, dull conditions and holds ligaments in place.

DEEP EMERALD GREEN burns, destroys and disperses diseased parts of the body when the very powerful and stronger Ray of *Purple* would be drastic.

PURPLE. Of intense power, used only in extreme cases to burn and destroy and after use the patient should rest for some time.

BLUE. These are building rays, used in conjunction with the burning rays of Emerald Green and Purple to build up, after the breaking down process has been accomplished. They are calming, soothing and very much used for allaying irritation and treatment of the Mental Body or Emotional Body and when the mind is unable to concentrate or has become confused.

MAUVE. Seldom used as a Ray, but more as a Force. Used physically, it can cause depression and frustration, and should never be used as it is too overpowering and has the reverse effect from that which is expected, unless the person using it is *capable* of receiving and adapting its force, by reason of Soul Evolution.

PINK. Part of the Red Ray, used both as a Ray and a Force. It is very helpful indeed in glandular and eye troubles. As a Force it conveys the intensity of the Love vibration. It relaxes, soothes and embraces the whole personality. It is used in its many varying shades according to the need.

INDIGO or BLUE BLACK. Deeply soothing. It calms intense nervous strain, painful elements in the body and headaches. It is very often used in conjunction with paler shades of other rays and green in particular.

BLACK and WHITE contain all colours and are extensively used for all conditions.

WHITE. For enfolding and clearing conditions before actual treatment commences. It is used in mental cases, breakdowns of all kinds, cleansing and purifying and also for lifting the vibrations of the Soul and Etheric body at the point of death.

BLACK. Deep and velvety—a beautiful force that calms, reassures and soothes in every way. It counteracts reaction of all kinds and promotes sleep and the relaxing of tensions.

PEARL RAY. Quite a unique ray and seldom used as it is contained within the body of a dedicated Healer, who has come to the Earth expressly to give Service and is therefore an advanced soul. It may only be released for very special work by one who is a Master, and is used for the evolving of a soul from a Karmic point of need. This is of course an exceedingly rare and beautiful force. It is released from the Solar Plexus of the Healer when used.

"We give Thee thanks, O giver of All gifts, for that most precious gift of Life that Thou has given to each one. We ask of Thee, that as thy Chelas walk Thy Way, with arms outstretched, with head upraised and feet placed firmly on the Path, that they shall ever touch all points of Light and stand for ever in the Circle of Thy Love. The Great Spirit Bless Thee and strengthen Thee and give thee Peace, all the days of thy Life."